D1421108

# COOK'S KITCHEN

# 30 MINUTE MEALS

igloobooks

Published in 2015
by Igloo Books Ltd
Cottage Farm
Sywell
NN6 0BJ
www.igloobooks.com

Food photography and recipe development: PhotoCuisine UK
Front and back cover images © PhotoCuisine UK

HUN001 0715
4 6 8 10 9 7 5
ISBN 978-1-78343-531-9

Printed and manufactured in China

# Contents

# Breakfast

# Pancakes with Bacon and Eggs

**SERVES 2**

**PREPARATION TIME 5 MINUTES**

**COOKING TIME 25 MINUTES**

## INGREDIENTS

250 g / 9 oz / 1 ⅔ cups plain (all purpose) flour

2 tsp baking powder

4 large eggs

300 ml / 10 ½ fl. oz / 1 ¼ cups milk

2 tbsp butter

2 rashers smoked streaky bacon

## METHOD

- Mix the flour and baking powder in a bowl and make a well in the centre. Break in 2 eggs and pour in the milk, then use a whisk to gradually incorporate all of the flour from round the outside.

- Melt the butter in a small frying pan then whisk it into the batter. Put the buttered frying pan back over a low heat. You will need a tablespoon of batter for each pancake and you should be able to cook 4 pancakes at a time in the frying pan.

- Spoon the batter into the pan and cook for 2 minutes or until small bubbles start to appear on the surface. Turn the pancakes over with a spatula and cook the other side until golden brown and cooked through.

- Repeat until all the batter has been used, keeping the finished batches warm in a low oven.

- Fry the remaining eggs and the bacon in a separate frying pan until the bacon is crisp and the egg whites have set.

- Divide the pancakes between 2 warm plates and top with the eggs and bacon.

**TOP TIP**

Fold 50 g of chopped cooked spinach through the batter before cooking.

# Scrambled Egg with Asparagus

**SERVES 4**

**PREPARATION TIME 2 MINUTES**

**COOKING TIME 5 MINUTES**

## INGREDIENTS

12 asparagus spears, cut into short lengths

8 large eggs

1 tbsp butter

pinch of salt

## METHOD

- Steam the asparagus for 4 minutes or until tender.

- Meanwhile, gently beat the eggs with a pinch of salt and pepper to break up the yolks.

- Heat the butter in a non-stick frying pan until sizzling then pour in the eggs. Cook over a low heat, stirring constantly until the eggs scramble.

- Stir in the asparagus and divide between 4 warm bowls. Serve immediately.

**TOP TIP**

Great for brunch if you don't have time for breakfast.

# Fruity Cereal

## SERVES 1

## PREPARATION TIME 5 MINUTES

## INGREDIENTS

15 g / ½ oz / ½ cup cereal flakes
2 tbsp dried apple pieces
3 strawberries, quartered
6 green grapes, halved
150 ml / 5 ½ fl. oz / ⅔ cup apple juice

## METHOD

- Mix the cereal, dried apple, strawberries and grapes together in a bowl.

- Pour over the apple juice and eat straight away.

**TOP TIP**
Sprinkle over 2 tbsp of crunchy granola for extra texture.

# Poached Eggs on Toast with Ham and Asparagus

RVES 4

EPARATION TIME 10 MINUTES

OKING TIME 5 MINUTES

## GREDIENTS

asparagus spears, trimmed

bsp white wine vinegar

large very fresh eggs

slices white bread

tbsp butter

slices honey roast ham

## METHOD

- Steam the asparagus for 5 minutes or until tender.

- Meanwhile, bring a wide saucepan of water to a gentle simmer and stir in the vinegar.

- Crack each egg into a cup and pour them smoothly into the water, one at a time. Poach gently for 3 minutes.

- Toast the bread lightly, then spread with the butter and top with the asparagus and ham. Lay a poached egg on top of each one and serve immediately.

**TOP TIP**

Try replacing the asparagus with purple sprouting broccoli.

# Banana and Cinnamon French Toast

**SERVES 4**

**PREPARATION TIME 10 MINUTES**

**COOKING TIME 6 MINUTES**

## INGREDIENTS

2 large eggs

75 ml / 2 ½ fl. oz / ⅓ cup whole milk

4 tbsp butter

4 thick slices sourdough bread

3 tbsp dark brown sugar

½ tsp ground cinnamon

2 bananas, sliced

cinnamon sticks to garnish

## METHOD

- Preheat the grill to its highest setting. Lightly beat the eggs with the milk in a wide, shallow dish. Heat half of the butter in a large frying pan until sizzling.

- Dip the sourdough slices in the egg mixture on both sides until evenly coated, then fry them in the butter for 2 minutes on each side or until golden brown.

- Meanwhile, gently heat the rest of the butter with the brown sugar and ground cinnamon in a small saucepan to melt the sugar.

- Transfer the French toast to a grill tray and top with the sliced bananas. Spoon over the brown sugar mixture and top each one with a cinnamon stick, then cook under the grill for 1–2 minutes to caramelise the top.

**TOP TIP**

Scatter over some honey-roasted almonds for added crunch.

# Bacon and Herb Omelette

**SERVES 1**

**PREPARATION TIME 2 MINUTES**

**COOKING TIME 6 MINUTES**

## INGREDIENTS

1 tbsp butter

1 rasher unsmoked back bacon, chopped

3 large eggs

1 tbsp flat leaf parsley, chopped

Salt and black pepper

## METHOD

- Heat the butter in a frying pan, then fry the bacon for 2 minutes. Remove it from the pan with a slotted spoon and reserve.

- Lightly beat the eggs with the parsley and a pinch of salt and pepper. Pour the mixture into the frying pan and cook over a medium heat until it starts to set around the outside.

- Use a spatula to draw the sides of the omelette into the centre then tilt the pan to fill the gaps with more liquid egg. Repeat the process until the top of the omelette is almost set then sprinkle over the bacon pieces.

- Fold the omelette in half and serve immediately.

**TOP TIP**

Replace the bacon with thinly sliced mushrooms.

# Smoked Salmon Scrambled Eggs

SERVES 1

PREPARATION TIME 10 MINUTES

COOKING TIME 4 MINUTES

## INGREDIENTS

2 large eggs

25 g / 1 oz / ⅛ cup smoked salmon, chopped

2 tsp crème fraiche

1 chive, cut into short lengths

sea salt

## METHOD

- Break the eggs into a small saucepan, retaining the bigger half of the shells. Carefully rinse and dry the egg shells, then sit them inside 2 egg cups.

- Gently beat the eggs in the saucepan with a pinch of salt.

- Turn on the heat under the pan and stir the eggs until they scramble, then spoon them back into their shells.

- Top each egg with smoked salmon and crème fraiche, then garnish with chives before serving.

**TOP TIP**
Top the finished eggs with a spoonful of caviar for a extra decadent treat.

# Poached Egg and Salad on Toast

SERVES 4

PREPARATION TIME 5 MINUTES

COOKING TIME 4 MINUTES

## INGREDIENTS

1 tbsp white wine vinegar

4 large very fresh eggs

4 slices granary bread

1 tbsp butter

4 tomatoes, quartered

mixed salad leaves to serve

salt and black pepper

## METHOD

- Bring a wide saucepan of water to a gentle simmer and stir in the vinegar.

- Crack each egg into a cup and pour them smoothly into the water, one at a time. Poach gently for 3 minutes.

- Toast the bread lightly, then spread with the butter and top with the tomatoes and salad leaves.

- Drain the eggs well, then sit them on top of the salad and sprinkle with salt and pepper.

## TOP TIP

Try topping the egg with a spoonful of Greek yoghurt and a sprinkle of chilli flakes.

# Fruity Rice Pudding

**SERVES 6**

**PREPARATION TIME 15 MINUTES**

**COOKING TIME 10 MINUTES**

## INGREDIENTS

110 g / 4 oz / ½ cup short grain rice

75 g / 2 ½ oz / ¼ cup runny honey

1.2 litres / 2 pints / 4 ½ cups whole milk

4 tbsp sultanas

1 red apple, cored, quartered and very
   thinly sliced

3 tbsp crème fraiche

250 g / 9 oz / 1 ⅔ cups mixed summer berries

2 tbsp sunflower seeds

## METHOD

- Stir the rice, honey, milk, sultanas
  and apple together in a microwavable
  bowl, then cover with cling film and
  pierce the top.

- Cook on high for 5 minutes, then
  stir well and cook for another 5
  minutes or until all the milk has been
  absorbed and the rice is tender. Leave
  to stand for 5 minutes.

- Divide the rice pudding between
  6 bowls and spoon a little crème
  fraiche on top. Scatter over the
  berries and sprinkle with sunflower
  seeds before serving.

**TOP TIP**

This rice pudding also tastes great chilled if you make it in advance.

# Banana and Hazelnut Pancakes

SERVES 4

PREPARATION TIME 5 MINUTES

COOKING TIME 20 MINUTES

## INGREDIENTS

250 g / 9 oz / 1 ⅔ cups plain (all purpose) flour

1 tsp baking powder

4 large eggs

300 ml / 10 ½ fl. oz / 1 ¼ cups milk

2 tbsp butter

2 bananas, sliced

4 tbsp Greek yoghurt

4 tbsp toasted hazelnuts (cobnuts), chopped

## METHOD

- Mix the flour and baking powder in a bowl and make a well in the centre. Break in the eggs and pour in the milk, then use a whisk to gradually incorporate all of the flour from round the outside.

- Melt the butter in a small frying pan then whisk it into the batter. Put the buttered frying pan back over a low heat. You will need a tablespoon of batter for each pancake and you should be able to cook 4 pancakes at a time in the frying pan. Spoon the batter into the pan and drop a few slices of banana on top of each one.

- Cook for 2 minutes or until small bubbles start to appear on the surface. Turn the pancakes over with a spatula and cook the other side until golden brown and cooked through.

- Repeat until all the batter has been used, keeping the finished batches warm in a low oven. Pile the pancakes onto warm plates and top each one with a spoonful of Greek yoghurt, the rest of the sliced banana and a sprinkle of hazelnuts.

**TOP TIP**
Try replacing the hazelnuts with pecan nuts and add a drizzle of maple syrup.

27

# Brown Sugar Porridge

**SERVES 1**

**PREPARATION TIME 5 MINUTES**

**COOKING TIME 7 MINUTES**

## INGREDIENTS

50 ml / 1 ¾ fl. oz / ¼ cup whole milk, plus
    extra to serve
40 g / 1 ½ oz / ½ cup oatmeal
1 tbsp brown sugar

## METHOD

- Bring the milk and 100 ml / 3 ½ fl. oz / ½ cup of water to the boil, then stir in the oatmeal and a pinch of salt.

- Simmer the porridge over a low heat for 5–6 minutes, stirring occasionally. Add a little more water if it gets too thick.

- Turn off the heat, cover the pan and leave the porridge to stand for 1 minute.

- Spoon the porridge into a bowl and stir in the brown sugar. Top up with a little more milk if you prefer a thinner consistency.

**TOP TIP**

Try topping the porridge with a sliced banana or a handful of blueberries.

# Melon with Prosciutto Grissini

SERVES 4

PREPARATION TIME 25 MINUTES

## INGREDIENTS

small orange-fleshed melons
seedless watermelon
osp white port
me sprigs to garnish
rissini
ices prosciutto, halved

## METHOD

- Cut the tops off 4 of the melons in a zigzag pattern and scrape out the seeds with a spoon. Cut a small slice off the bases so that they stand upright without wobbling.

- Cut the other melon in half and discard the seeds, then use a melon baller to scoop the flesh into spheres. Do the same with the watermelon, then pile the melon balls into the prepared melons. Spoon over the port and garnish with thyme.

- Wrap the end of each grissini with half a slice of prosciutto and serve with the melons.

**TOP TIP**

You can also wrap the grissini with thinly sliced salami.

# Coddled Eggs with Morcilla

**SERVES 4**

**PREPARATION TIME 10 MINUTES**

**COOKING TIME 15 MINUTES**

## INGREDIENTS

150 ml / 5 ½ fl. oz / ⅔ cup crème fraiche

4 large eggs

8 slices morcilla, or black pudding

½ tsp cumin seeds

2 slices bread

salt and black pepper

## METHOD

- Preheat the oven to 180°C (160°C fan) / 350F / gas 4.

- Season the crème fraiche well with salt and pepper and divide it between 4 mini casserole dishes. Make a well in the centre and crack an egg into each one. Top with the morcilla slices and a sprinkle of cumin seeds

- Sit the dishes in a roasting tin and pour enough boiling water around them to come halfway up the sides. Transfer the tin to the oven and bake for 15 minutes or until the whites of the eggs are set, but the yolks are still runny.

- Toast the bread and cut it into soldiers, then serve with the coddled eggs.

**TOP TIP**

If you can't find morcilla, black pudding makes a good alternative.

# Beef Carpaccio Crostini

MAKES 4

PREPARATION TIME 15 MINUTES

COOKING TIME 2 MINUTES

## INGREDIENTS

orange

slices sourdough bread

handful of mixed salad leaves

tbsp extra virgin olive oil

wafer-thin slices raw beef fillet

cooked beetroot, diced

tbsp flat leaf parsley, chopped

tbsp walnut pieces, chopped

salt

## METHOD

- Slice the top and bottom off the orange. Slice away the peel then cut out each individual segment, leaving the white pith behind like the pages of a book. Discard the pith.

- Toast the sourdough until crisp and golden brown, then leave to cool for 2 minutes before topping with the salad leaves.

- Massage the oil into the beef and season with a little salt, then arrange on top of the toast. Top with the orange segments and beetroot cubes and sprinkle with parsley and walnuts. Serve immediately.

**TOP TIP**

Shave over a little Parmesan with a vegetable peeler for a tangy finish.

# Preserved Vegetable and Prosciutto Crostini

**MAKES 2**

**PREPARATION TIME 5 MINUTES**

**COOKING TIME 2 MINUTES**

## INGREDIENTS

2 slices sourdough bread

1 clove of garlic, halved

1 tbsp extra virgin olive oil

4 slices chargrilled aubergine (eggplant) in oil, drained

4 strips roasted red pepper in oil, drained

4 thin slices prosciutto

2 tsp thyme, chopped

black pepper

## METHOD

- Toast the sourdough until crisp and golden brown, then rub it vigorously all over with the cut side of a garlic clove. Drizzle the toast with oil.

- Arrange the aubergine and pepper slices on top, then add the prosciutto and sprinkle with thyme and black pepper.

**TOP TIP**
Top the crostini with a few baby capers for a tangy finish.

# Melon, Ham and Grape Salad

## METHOD

- Use a melon baller to scoop the melon into spheres, then toss with the grapes, ham and lettuce.

- Divide between 4 bowls and dress with the vinegar then season with salt and pepper.

RVES 4

REPARATION TIME 2 MINUTES

## INGREDIENTS

orange-fleshed melon

0 g / 5 ½ oz / 1 cup green seedless grapes, halved

0 g / 5 ½ oz / ⅔ cup honey roast ham, sliced

g / 1 ¾ oz / 2 cups lamb's lettuce

bsp white balsamic vinegar

lt and black pepper

**TOP TIP**

Top the salad with roasted salted almonds for added crunch.

# Pancakes with Raspberries and Honey

SERVES 2

PREPARATION TIME 5 MINUTES

COOKING TIME 25 MINUTES

## INGREDIENTS

250 g / 9 oz / 1 ⅔ cups plain (all purpose) flour

2 tsp baking powder

2 large eggs

300 ml / 10 ½ fl. oz / 1 ¼ cups milk

2 tbsp butter

4 tbsp runny honey

50 g / 1 ¾ oz / ⅔ cup raspberries

## METHOD

- Mix the flour and baking powder in a bowl and make a well in the centre. Break in the eggs and pour in the milk, then use a whisk to gradually incorporate all of the flour from round the outside.

- Melt the butter in a frying pan, then whisk it into the batter. Put the buttered frying pan back over a low heat. You will need a tablespoon of batter for each pancake and you should be able to cook 4 pancakes at a time in the frying pan.

- Spoon the batter into the pan and cook for 2 minutes or until small bubbles start to appear on the surface. Turn the pancakes over with a spatula and cook the other side until golden brown and cooked through.

- Repeat until all the batter has been used, keeping the finished batches warm in a low oven.

- Pile the pancakes onto 2 warm plates and drizzle with the honey. Break the raspberries into small pieces with your fingers and scatter over the top.

**TOP TIP**

Add a few drops of rose water to the pancake batter for a floral aroma.

# Eggs Poached in Tomato Sauce

SERVES 2

PREPARATION TIME 2 MINUTES

COOKING TIME 10 MINUTES

## INGREDIENTS

2 tbsp olive oil

1 onion, finely chopped

2 cloves of garlic, crushed

300 ml / 10 ½ fl. oz / 1 ¼ cups tomato passata

3 large eggs

4 tbsp Parmesan shavings

4 tbsp flat leaf parsley, shredded

salt and black pepper

## METHOD

- Heat the oil in a frying pan and fry the onion and garlic for 5 minutes without colouring. Stir in the passata and season with salt and pepper, then bring to a simmer.

- Crack in the eggs, then reduce the heat. Put on the lid and poach gently for 4 minutes or until the whites are set, but the yolks are still a little runny.

- Sprinkle with Parmesan and parsley and serve immediately.

**TOP TIP**

Try topping the finished dish with a little Greek yoghurt and a sprinkle of chilli flakes.

# Marinated Melon

## SERVES 4

## PREPARATION TIME 30 MINUTES

## INGREDIENTS

1 white-fleshed melon
½ seedless watermelon
4 tbsp melon liqueur

## METHOD

- Cut the white-fleshed melon in half and scoop out the seeds. Cut it into wedges, then cut away and discard the rind. Cut the flesh into bite-sized chunks.

- Cut off the discard the rind of the watermelon, then cut the flesh into chunk and mix with the rest of the melon.

- Spoon over the melon liqueur and leave to marinate for 15 minutes before serving.

**TOP TIP**
Sprinkle the melon with chopped pistachio nuts just before serving.

# Lunches

# Speedy Eggs Benedict

---

**SERVES 2**

**PREPARATION TIME 15 MINUTES**

**COOKING TIME 4 MINUTES**

---

## INGREDIENTS

4 large eggs

2 bread rolls, halved

4 slices honey-roast ham

1 tbsp lemon juice

1 tbsp French tarragon, chopped

3 tbsp mayonnaise

2 tbsp whipped cream

## METHOD

- Bring a large pan of water to a simmer. Oil a sheet of cling film and lay it, oil side up, in a mug. Break in an egg, then draw up the sides and twist them together to make a waterproof package. Repeat with 3 more sheets of cling film and the other eggs.

- Lower the eggs into the simmering water and poach gently for 4 minutes.

- Toast the rolls and lay a slice of ham on top of each half.

- Stir the lemon juice and tarragon into the mayonnaise and fold in the whipped cream.

- When the eggs are ready, remove and discard the cling film and lay them on top of the ham. Serve with the mayonnaise mixture on the side for spooning over at the table.

**TOP TIP**

Replace the ham with smoked salmon to make speedy eggs royale.

# Goats' Cheese and Prosciutto Bagels

SERVES 2

PREPARATION TIME 5 MINUTES

COOKING TIME 2 MINUTES

## INGREDIENTS

slices goats' cheese log

tsp thyme leaves

seeded bagels, split in half

tbsp olive oil

slices prosciutto

## METHOD

- Preheat the grill to its highest setting.

- Spread the goats' cheese slices out on a baking tray and sprinkle with thyme. Cook under the grill for 2 minutes or until the top of the cheese is lightly toasted.

- Drizzle the bagel halves with oil, then arrange the prosciutto slices on top of the bottoms and position the toasted goats' cheese on top. Place the bagel tops on top and serve immediately.

**TOP TIP**
Try adding some sun-blushed tomatoes for a tangy flavour.

# Scrambled Egg with Rocket

## METHOD

- Gently beat the eggs with a pinch of salt and pepper to break up the yolks.

- Heat the butter in a non-stick frying pan until sizzling then pour in the eggs. Cook over a low heat, stirring constantly until the eggs scramble.

- Stir in half of the rocket then spoon it over the muffin halves.

- Serve with extra rocket leaves on the side and a sprinkle of black pepper.

**SERVES 4**

**PREPARATION TIME 2 MINUTES**

**COOKING TIME 5 MINUTES**

## INGREDIENTS

8 large eggs

2 tbsp butter

50 g / 1 ¾ oz / 1 cup rocket (arugula) leaves

4 English breakfast muffins, halved and toasted

salt and black pepper

**TOP TIP**

Stir 100 g of cubed pan-fried chorizo into the eggs when you add the rocket.

# Chicken and Apple Salad

**RVES 2**

**REPARATION TIME 5 MINUTES**

**OKING TIME 6 MINUTES**

## GREDIENTS

hicken breasts

Granny Smith apple, cored and quartered

emon, halved

arge carrot, grated

g / 2 ½ oz / ¾ cup cheese, cubed

bsp sultanas

handful of lamb's lettuce

piece wholemeal toast

lt and black pepper

## METHOD

- Preheat the grill to its highest setting.

- Season the chicken with salt and pepper, then grill for 3 minutes on each side or until golden brown and cooked through.

- Thinly slice the apple, then squeeze over the lemon juice to stop it from going brown.

- Slice the chicken breasts and arrange them in 2 bowls with the apple, carrot, cheese, sultanas and lettuce. Tear the toast into rustic croutons and scatter over the top.

**TOP TIP**

Try topping the salad with a sprinkle of chopped walnuts for added crunch.

# Monkfish and Sesame Seed Skewers

**SERVES 2**

**PREPARATION TIME 20 MINUTES**

**COOKING TIME 6 MINUTES**

## INGREDIENTS

2 tbsp runny honey

1 tbsp lemon juice

1 tsp mild curry powder

225 g / 8 oz / 1 cup monkfish tail fillet, cubed

2 tbsp sesame seeds

1 tbsp flat leaf parsley, finely chopped

salt and black pepper

## METHOD

- Mix the honey, lemon juice and curry powder together and season with salt and pepper. Pour the mixture over the monkfish and leave to marinate for 15 minutes.

- Meanwhile, soak 6 wooden skewers in a bowl of cold water.

- Preheat the grill to its highest setting. Thread the monkfish onto the skewers and sprinkle with sesame seeds.

- Cook the skewers under the grill for 6 minutes, turning occasionally, or until the fish is only just cooked in the centre. Sprinkle with parsley and serve immediately.

**TOP TIP**

This recipe also works well with prawns or lobster.

# Duck Skewers with Lemon Courgettes

SERVES 2

PREPARATION TIME 15 MINUTES

COOKING TIME 6 MINUTES

## INGREDIENTS

- tbsp chilli (chili) jam
- tbsp dark soy sauce
- duck breasts, skinned and halved lengthways
- courgette (zucchini), cut into thick slices
- lemon, halved

## METHOD

- Stir the chilli jam and soy together then massage it into the duck breasts. Leave to marinate for 10 minutes.

- Preheat a griddle pan until smoking hot.

- Thread the duck lengthways onto 4 skewers, then griddle for 3 minutes on each side or until nicely marked, but still pink in the centre.

- Meanwhile, steam the courgette slices for 4 minutes. Squeeze the lemon over the courgette, then serve with the duck skewers.

**TOP TIP**
This recipe also works well with lamb neck fillet.

# Herb Omelette with Sun-blush Tomatoes

**SERVES 1**

**PREPARATION TIME 5 MINUTES**

**COOKING TIME 6 MINUTES**

## INGREDIENTS

1 tbsp butter

2 large eggs

1 tbsp flat leaf parsley, finely chopped

1 tbsp chives, finely chopped

50 g / 1 ¾ oz / ½ cup sun-blush tomatoes
   in oil, drained and quartered

2 anchovy fillets, chopped

1 tsp capers, in brine, drained

salt and black pepper

## METHOD

- Heat the butter in a frying pan. Lightly beat the eggs with the herbs and a pinch of salt and pepper.

- Pour the mixture into the frying pan and cook over a medium heat until it starts to set around the outside.

- Use a spatula to draw the sides of the omelette into the centre then tilt the pan to fill the gaps with more liquid egg. Repeat the process until the top of the omelette is almost set then turn it over and cook the other side.

- Slide the omelette onto a chopping board and slice it into thick ribbons. Arrange the omelette with the tomatoes, anchovy and capers on a warm plate and serve immediately.

**TOP TIP**

Replace some of the sunblush tomatoes with any antipasti – try olives or artichokes.

# Poached Egg and Bacon Baps

SERVES 4

PREPARATION TIME 2 MINUTES

COOKING TIME 5 MINUTES

## INGREDIENTS

thick rashers streaky bacon
very fresh eggs
sesame baps
lettuce leaves
large tomato, sliced
new potatoes and salad to serve

## METHOD

- Preheat the grill to its highest setting and bring a wide saucepan of water to a gentle simmer.

- Grill the bacon for 2 minutes on each side or until crisp and golden brown.

- Meanwhile, crack each egg into a cup and pour them smoothly into the water, one at a time.

- Simmer gently for 3 minutes. Slice the baps in half and add a lettuce leaf and a thick slice of tomato to the bottom halves.

- Top the tomato with the bacon. Use a slotted spoon to take the eggs out of the water and blot the underneath on a piece of kitchen paper before laying them on top of the bacon.

- Put the lids on the baps and hold everything together with a wooden skewer, then serve with new potatoes and salad.

**TOP TIP**
Replace the tomato sliced with chargilled red peppers in oil.

# Spiced Turkey Kebabs

## SERVES 4

## PREPARATION TIME 20 MINUTES

## COOKING TIME 8 MINUTES

## INGREDIENTS

2 tbsp chilli (chili) jam (jelly)

1 tbsp mild curry powder

450 g / 1 lb / 2 cups turkey breast, cut
    into chunks

1 yellow pepper, deseeded and cut
    into chunks

1 red onion, cut into rings

2 tomatoes, peeled, deseeded and diced

½ cucumber, peeled, deseeded and diced

1 tbsp vegetable oil

1 tbsp lemon juice

1 tsp Worcestershire sauce

## METHOD

- Stir the chilli jam and curry powder
  together then massage it into the turkey
  and pepper. Leave to marinate for
  10 minutes.

- Preheat a griddle pan until smoking hot

- Thread the turkey and pepper onto
  4 skewers, then griddle with the onion
  rings for 4 minutes on each side or until
  nicely marked and cooked through.

- Meanwhile, mix the tomato and
  cucumber together and dress with the
  oil, lemon juice and Worcestershire sauce

- Serve the kebabs and onion rings with
  the tomato and cucumber salad on
  the side.

**TOP TIP**

This recipe also works
well with pork in place
of the turkey.

# Coconut Pancakes with Sweet and Sour Tuna

**RVES 4**

**EPARATION TIME 5 MINUTES**

**OKING TIME 25 MINUTES**

## GREDIENTS

0 g / 9 oz / 1 ⅔ cups plain (all purpose) flour

sp baking powder

arge eggs

0 ml / 10 ½ fl. oz / 1 ¼ cups coconut milk

bsp butter

bsp desiccated coconut

### R THE TUNA

g / 1 ¾ oz / ¼ cup brown sugar

ml / 1 ¾ fl. oz / ¼ cup rice wine vinegar

0 g / 5 ½ oz / ½ cup tomato ketchup

0 g / 5 ½ oz / 1 cup canned pineapple
chunks in juice

0 g / 5 ½ oz / 1 cup canned white tuna in
oil, drained

bsp flat leaf parsley, chopped

## METHOD

- First make the tuna. Put all of the ingredients, except the tuna and parsley in a small saucepan and simmer for 5 minutes. Stir in the tuna and keep warm.

- Meanwhile, mix the flour and baking powder in a bowl and make a well in the centre. Break in the eggs and pour in the coconut milk, then use a whisk to gradually incorporate all of the flour from round the outside.

- Melt the butter in a small frying pan then whisk it into the batter with the desiccated coconut. Put the buttered frying pan back over a low heat. You will need a tablespoon of batter for each pancake and you should be able to cook 4 pancakes at a time in the frying pan.

- Spoon the batter into the pan and cook for 2 minutes or until small bubbles start to appear on the surface. Turn the pancakes over with a spatula and cook the other side until golden brown and cooked through.

- Repeat until all the batter has been used, keeping the finished batches warm in a low oven. Serve the pancakes on warm plates with the tuna spooned over and sprinkle with parsley.

**TOP TIP**

Add a sprinkle of roughly chopped cashew nuts for added crunch.

# Salad Tacos

**SERVES 4**

**PREPARATION TIME 5 MINUTES**

## INGREDIENTS

4 plain flour tortillas

¼ iceberg lettuce, shredded

4 tomatoes, diced

1 onion, finely chopped

3 tbsp coriander (cilantro) leaves, finely chopped

2 tbsp olive oil

1 tbsp lime juice

4 tbsp soured cream

salt and black pepper

## METHOD

- Lay the tortillas out on a chopping board and divide the lettuce between them.

- Mix the tomato, onion, coriander and oil together and season with salt and pepper. Spoon the mixture on top of the lettuce.

- Stir the lime juice into the soured cream, then drizzle it over the salsa, fold the tortillas in half and serve.

**TOP TIP**
These tacos can be topped with pan-fried pieces of chicken, steak or chorizo.

# Chickpea Pancakes with Tabbouleh

**SERVES 4**

**PREPARATION TIME 10 MINUTES**

**COOKING TIME 20 MINUTES**

## INGREDIENTS

- 250 g / 9 oz / 1 ⅔ cups gram flour
- 1 tsp baking powder
- 2 large eggs
- 300 ml / 10 ½ fl. oz / 1 ¼ cups milk
- 1 tbsp butter

### FOR THE TABBOULEH

- 150 g / 5 ½ oz / ¾ cup bulgar wheat
- 1 small bunch flat leaf parsley, finely chopped
- 2 tomatoes, deseeded and finely chopped
- 2 shallots, finely chopped
- 1 lemon, juiced
- 2 tbsp extra virgin olive oil
- salt and black pepper

## METHOD

- Put the bulgar wheat in a bowl and pour over enough boiling water to just cover it. Cover the bowl with cling film and leave to soak for 15 minutes.

- Meanwhile, mix the gram flour and baking powder in a bowl and make a well in the centre. Break in the eggs and pour in the milk then use a whisk to gradually incorporate all of the flour from round the outside.

- Melt the butter in a small frying pan then whisk it into the batter. Put the buttered frying pan back over a low heat. You will need a tablespoon of batter for each pancake and you should be able to cook 4 pancakes at a time in the frying pan. Spoon the batter into the pan and cook for 2 minutes or until small bubbles start to appear on the surface. Turn the pancakes over with a spatula and cook the other side until golden brown and cooked through.

- Repeat until all the batter has been used, keeping the finished batches warm in a low oven.

- Tip the bulgar wheat into a sieve and run it under the cold tap to cool. Drain well. Stir the parsley, tomato and shallot into the bulgar and dress with the lemon juice and olive oil.

- Season with salt and pepper then serve with the pancakes.

**TOP TIP**

Spread with hummus and top with spicy merguez sausage.

# Carrot and Turkey Soup

## METHOD

- Heat the oil and butter in a saucepan and fry the onion for 5 minutes or until softened.

- Add the garlic, carrots and cumin to the pan and cook for 2 more minutes, then stir in the stock and bring to the boil.

- Simmer for 15 minutes or until the carrots are tender. Ladle the soup into a liquidiser and blend until smooth then season to taste with salt and pepper.

- Divide the soup between 4 warm bowls and stir a little crème fraiche into each one. Top with the turkey and garnish with dill.

**SERVES 4**

**PREPARATION TIME 5 MINUTES**

**COOKING TIME 25 MINUTES**

## INGREDIENTS

2 tbsp olive oil

2 tbsp butter

1 onion, finely chopped

2 cloves of garlic, crushed

4 carrots, diced

½ tsp ground cumin, plus extra to sprinkle

1 litre / 1 pint 15 fl. oz / 4 cups turkey stock

4 tbsp crème fraiche

4 wafer thin slices turkey, sliced

dill sprigs to garnish

salt and black pepper

**TOP TIP**

Try replacing the turkey with smoked salmon and garnish the soup with fresh dill.

# Sardines Wrapped in Bacon

SERVES 2

PREPARATION TIME 10 MINUTES

COOKING TIME 6 MINUTES

## INGREDIENTS

boneless sardine fillets

sprigs rosemary

tbsp pine nuts

rashers unsmoked streaky bacon

## METHOD

- Preheat the grill to its highest setting.

- Top each sardine fillet with a sprig of rosemary and a tablespoon of pine nuts, then wrap tightly with bacon and secure with cocktail sticks.

- Grill the sardine parcels for 3 minutes on each side or until the bacon is golden and crisp and the fish is just cooked in the centre. Serve immediately.

**TOP TIP**
This recipe also works really well with mackerel fillets.

# Bacon, Potato and Spinach Frittata

## SERVES 4

**PREPARATION TIME 10 MINUTES**

**COOKING TIME 12 MINUTES**

### INGREDIENTS

150 g / 5 ½ oz / ¾ cup thin-cut smoked bacon, chopped

a large handful baby leaf spinach, chopped

75 g / 2 ½ oz / ½ cup boiled potatoes, cubed

6 large eggs, lightly beaten

1 tbsp butter

salt and black pepper

## METHOD

- Preheat the grill to its highest setting.

- Stir the bacon, spinach and potatoes into the eggs and season with salt and pepper.

- Melt the butter in an oven-proof frying pan then pour in the egg mixture and cook over a gentle heat for 6–8 minutes or until the egg has set around the outside.

- Put the frying pan under the grill to cook the top for 3–4 minutes or until golden brown and just set. Serve immediately.

**TOP TIP**

Try replacing the bacon with chorizo for a spicy kick.

# Sweetcorn Pancakes with Roasted Tomatoes

**SERVES 4**

**PREPARATION TIME 5 MINUTES**

**COOKING TIME 25 MINUTES**

## INGREDIENTS

250 g / 9 oz / 1 ⅔ cups plain (all purpose) flour

1 tsp baking powder

3 large eggs

300 ml / 10 ½ fl. oz / 1 ¼ cups milk

1 tbsp butter

200 g / 7 oz / 1 cup canned sweetcorn, drained

4 spring onions (scallions), finely chopped

1 tbsp olive oil

2 tomato vines

salad leaves to serve

salt and black pepper

## METHOD

- Preheat the oven to 190°C (170°C fan) / 375F / gas 5.

- Mix the flour and baking powder in a bowl and make a well in the centre. Break in the eggs and pour in the milk, then use a whisk to gradually incorporate all of the flour from round the outside.

- Melt the butter in a small frying pan then whisk it into the batter with the sweetcorn and spring onions. Put the buttered frying pan back over a low heat. You will need a tablespoon of batter for each pancake and you should be able to cook 4 pancakes at a time in the frying pan.

- Spoon the batter into the pan and cook for 2 minutes or until small bubbles start to appear on the surface. Turn the pancakes over with a spatula and cook the other side until golden brown and cooked through.

- Repeat until all the batter has been used, keeping the finished batches warm.

- While the pancakes are cooking drizzle the tomatoes with oil and roast on their vines for 10 minutes. Season with salt and pepper.

- Serve the pancakes with the roast tomatoes and some fresh salad leaves.

**TOP TIP**

Serve with slices of pan-fried chorizo for a spicy kick.

# Rigatoni with Broccoli and Lardons

**SERVES 4**

**PREPARATION TIME 5 MINUTES**

**COOKING TIME 12 MINUTES**

## INGREDIENTS

400 g / 14 oz / 3 ½ cups dried rigatoni

100 g / 3 ½ oz / 1 cup tenderstem broccoli

2 tbsp olive oil

100 g / 3 ½ oz / ½ cup lardons

1 lemon, zest finely pared

a handful of basil leaves

sea salt

## METHOD

- Cook the rigatoni in boiling, salted water according to the packet instructions or until al dente. 4 minutes before the end of the cooking time, add the broccoli to the pan. Drain well.

- While the pasta is cooking, heat the oil in a frying pan and fry the lardons for 4 minutes or until golden brown.

- Toss the pasta and broccoli with the lardons, then transfer to a warm serving dish and garnish with lemon zest and basil leaves.

**TOP TIP**
This recipe tastes great with any pasta shapes – try penne or fusilli.

# Spinach and Smoked Salmon Frittata

## SERVES 4

**PREPARATION TIME 5 MINUTES**

**COOKING TIME 12 MINUTES**

## INGREDIENTS

- tbsp butter
- large eggs, lightly beaten
- tbsp crème fraiche
- 0 g / 5 ½ oz / ¾ cup smoked salmon
- large handful baby leaf spinach
- few chives, cut into short lengths
- black pepper

## METHOD

- Preheat the grill to its highest setting.

- Melt the butter in an oven-proof frying pan. Pour in the eggs and cook over a gentle heat for 6–8 minutes or until the egg has set around the outside.

- Put the frying pan under the grill to cook the top for 3–4 minutes or until golden brown and just set.

- Spoon over the crème fraiche and arrange the smoked salmon on top. Scatter over the spinach and chives and serve immediately, sprinkled with black pepper.

**TOP TIP**

This recipe is delicious made with fresh crab meat in place of the smoked salmon.

83

# Fusilli with Pesto and Tomatoes

## SERVES 4
## PREPARATION TIME 5 MINUTES
## COOKING TIME 12 MINUTES

## INGREDIENTS

400 g / 14 oz / 4 cups dried fusilli

100 g / 3 ½ oz / ½ cup pesto

100 g / 3 ½ oz / ⅔ cup cherry tomatoes, quartered

2 tbsp black olives, chopped

50 g / 1 ¾ oz / ½ cup piece of Parmesan

sea salt

## METHOD

- Cook the pasta in boiling, salted water according to the packet instructions or until al dente.

- Drain well, then stir in the pesto and toss with the cherry tomatoes and olives.

- Divide the pasta between 4 warm bowls, then use a vegetable peeler to shave some Parmesan over each one.

**TOP TIP**

Sprinkle the pasta with toasted pine nuts for added crunch.

# Crispy Chicken Salad

**SERVES 5**

**PREPARATION TIME 15 MINUTES**

**COOKING TIME 4 MINUTES**

## INGREDIENTS

Sunflower oil for deep-frying

50 g / 2 ½ oz / ½ cup dried breadcrumbs

1 tbsp basil leaves, finely chopped

1 tbsp Parmesan, finely grated

4 skinless chicken breasts, cut into
bite-sized pieces

1 tbsp plain (all purpose) flour

1 large egg, beaten

100 g / 3 ½ oz / 2 cups baby leaf spinach

4 hard-boiled eggs, quartered

1 red pepper, quartered and thinly sliced

4 tbsp olive oil

1 tbsp lemon juice

1 tsp runny honey

Salt and black pepper

## METHOD

- Heat the sunflower oil in a deep
  fat fryer to 180°C, according to the
  manufacturer's instructions.

- Mix the breadcrumbs with the basil
  and Parmesan and spread them out
  on a plate.

- Dust the chicken breast pieces with
  flour, then dip them in egg and roll in
  the breadcrumb mixture to coat.

- Fry the chicken pieces for 4 minutes
  or until golden brown and cooked
  through. Drain well on absorbent paper.

- Arrange the spinach leaves on 4 plates
  and top with the chicken, egg and sliced
  pepper. Whisk together the olive oil,
  lemon juice and honey and season to
  taste with salt and pepper, then drizzle
  it over the salad.

**TOP TIP**
Use chicken thigh
instead of chicken
breast for an extra
juicy texture.

# Club Sandwich

**SERVES 1**

**PREPARATION TIME 5 MINUTES**

**COOKING TIME 4 MINUTES**

## INGREDIENTS

3 slices white bread, crusts removed

4 rashers smoked streaky bacon

4 slices cheese

½ cooked chicken breast, sliced

a handful of rocket (arugula)

## METHOD

- Preheat the grill to its highest setting. Grill the bread and bacon for 2 minutes, then turn everything over and top 2 of the bread slices with cheese. Grill for 2 more minutes or until the bacon is crisp and the cheese has melted.

- Top one of the cheese toasts with 2 rashers of the bacon, half of the chicken and half of the rocket.

- Top with the second cheese toast and top with the rest of the bacon, chicken and rocket. Press the plain slice of toast firmly on top, then cut in half diagonally and secure each half together with a cocktail stick.

**TOP TIP**

Add a sliced avocado to the sandwich for a buttery-smooth texture.

# Chorizo, Mozzarella and Sun-dried Tomato Rolls

SERVES 4

PREPARATION TIME 5 MINUTES

COOKING TIME 10 MINUTES

## INGREDIENTS

cheese baton rolls

4 tsp pesto

50 g / 1 ¾ oz / ¼ cup sun-dried tomatoes in oil, drained

2 balls light mozzarella, cubed

50 g / 1 ¾ oz / ¼ cup chorizo, thinly sliced

## METHOD

- Preheat the oven to 180°C (160°C fan) / 350F / gas 4.

- Cut the rolls in half lengthways and spread one side of each one with pesto.

- Drain the sun-dried tomatoes and layer them up in the rolls with the mozzarella and chorizo.

- Wrap each baton in foil and bake for 10 minutes to melt the cheese. Serve warm.

**TOP TIP**

For a vegetarian alternative, replace the chorizo with pitted green olives.

# Cheese and Sun-dried Tomato Rice Salad

**SERVES 4**

**PREPARATION TIME 10 MINUTES**

**COOKING TIME 20 MINUTES**

## INGREDIENTS

200 g / 7 oz / 1 cup long grain rice

1 tbsp runny honey

½ lemon, juiced

150 g / 5 ½ oz / ¾ cup reduced-fat hard
    cheese, cubed

100 g / 3 ½ oz / ¾ cup sun-dried tomatoes in
    oil, drained and chopped

2 tbsp chives, chopped

salt and black pepper

## METHOD

- Put the rice in a saucepan and add enou
  water to cover it by 1 cm (½ in).

- Bring the pan to the boil then cover an
  turn down the heat to its lowest setting

- Cook for 10 minutes then turn off the h
  and leave to stand, without lifting the li
  for 10 minutes.

- Whisk the honey with the lemon juice
  to make a dressing and season with salt
  and pepper.

- When the rice is ready, stir in the dressi
  cheese and tomatoes and garnish with
  chopped chives.

**TOP TIP**

Stir through a handful
of toasted pine nuts for
added crunch.

# Melon Gazpacho

## METHOD

- Scoop the flesh out of the melon into a liquidiser and add the cucumber, vinegar and oil.

- Blend until smooth, then pass the mixture through a sieve and season to taste with salt and pepper.

- Pour into 4 bowls and garnish with mint leaves.

**VES 4**

**PARATION TIME 10 MINUTES**

## REDIENTS

ge orange-fleshed melon, halved and eseeded

ucumber, peeled and diced

sp sherry vinegar

sp extra virgin olive oil

t leaves to garnish

and black pepper

**TOP TIP**
Try topping the gazpacho with crumbled feta for a tangy finish.

# Tomatoes Stuffed with Goats' Cheese

**SERVES 2**

**PREPARATION TIME 20 MINUTES**

**COOKING TIME 30 SECONDS**

## INGREDIENTS

6 medium tomatoes

400 g / 14 oz / 1 ¾ cups soft goats' cheese

1 lemon, zest finely grated

2 tbsp flat leaf parsley, finely chopped

2 tbsp chives, finely chopped

2 tbsp basil leaves, finely chopped

extra herbs to garnish

salt and black pepper

## METHOD

- Score a cross in the top of each tomato, then blanch them in boiling water for 30 seconds. Plunge into iced water, then peel off the skins.

- Cut a small slice from one side of each tomato. Use a melon baller to remove the core and seeds of the tomatoes.

- Mix the goats' cheese with the lemon zest and herbs and season to taste with salt and pepper.

- Pack the goats' cheese mixture into the tomatoes, then serve immediately, garnished with extra herbs.

**TOP TIP**
Try using the goats' cheese mixture to stuff fresh figs when they're in season.

# Cream of Mushroom Soup

## SERVES 4

### PREPARATION TIME 5 MINUTES

### COOKING TIME 25 MINUTES

## INGREDIENTS

- tsp olive oil
- tsp butter
- onion, finely chopped
- cloves of garlic, crushed
- g / 14 oz / 5 ⅓ cups flat cap mushrooms, chopped
- tre / 1 pint 15 fl. oz / 4 cups vegetable stock
- ml / 3 ½ fl. oz / ½ cup double (heavy) cream, plus extra to garnish
- ch of grated nutmeg
- pped flat leaf parsley to garnish
- and black pepper

## METHOD

- Heat the oil and butter in a saucepan and fry the onion for 5 minutes or until softened.

- Add the garlic and mushrooms to the pan and cook for 5 more minutes, then stir in the vegetable stock and bring to the boil.

- Simmer for 15 minutes then stir in the double cream and nutmeg.

- Blend the soup until smooth with a liquidiser or stick blender then taste for seasoning and adjust with salt and pepper.

- Ladle into warm mugs, then add a swirl of cream and a sprinkle of parsley to each one.

**TOP TIP**

Add 2 tbsp of chopped thyme leaves when you cook the garlic.

# Lentil and Sweet Potato Soup

**SERVES 4**

**PREPARATION TIME 5 MINUTES**

**COOKING TIME 25 MINUTES**

## INGREDIENTS

400 g / 14 oz / 3 ¼ cups red lentils
1 small sweet potato, peeled and diced
2 cloves of garlic, crushed
1 tbsp fresh root ginger, finely chopped
2 tsp mild curry powder
1.2 litres / 2 pints / 5 cups vegetable stock
2 tbsp crème fraiche
coriander (cilantro) to garnish
salt and black pepper

## METHOD

- Put the lentils, sweet potato, garlic, ginger, curry powder and vegetable stock in a saucepan and bring to the boil. Turn down the heat and simmer for 25 minutes or until the lentils and potato are completely tender.

- Transfer the soup to a liquidiser and blend until smooth. Season to taste with salt and pepper.

- Ladle the soup into warm bowls and top with a spoonful of crème fraiche and a sprinkle of coriander.

**TOP TIP**
The sweet potatoes can be replaced with butternut squash.

# Orzo Pasta with Rocket and Parmesan

SERVES 2

PREPARATION TIME 5 MINUTES

COOKING TIME 10 MINUTES

## INGREDIENTS

- g / 7 oz / 1 cup dried orzo pasta
- g / 1 ¾ oz / 1 cup rocket (arugula), chopped
- sp pesto
- sp Parmesan shavings
- salt and black pepper

## METHOD

- Cook the orzo in a large pan of boiling salted water according to the packet instructions or until al dente.

- Drain well, then stir in the rocket and pesto. Season to taste with salt and pepper.

- Divide the pasta between 2 bowls and scatter over the Parmesan shavings.

**TOP TIP**

For a gluten-free alternative, use basmati rice instead of the orzo pasta.

# Scallop Gratin

**SERVES 4**

**PREPARATION TIME 15 MINUTES**

**COOKING TIME 15 MINUTES**

## INGREDIENTS

12 scallops in the half shell, cleaned

2 tbsp butter

1 shallot, finely chopped

1 clove of garlic, crushed

1 tbsp plain (all purpose) flour

150 ml / 5 ½ fl. oz / ⅔ cup dry white wine

300 ml / 10 ½ fl. oz / 1 ¼ cups whole milk

a little freshly grated nutmeg

2 tbsp dried breadcrumbs

3 tbsp Gruyère cheese, grated

salt and black pepper

## METHOD

- Preheat the oven to 190°C (170°C fan) / 375F / gas 5.

- Carefully slice the scallops away from their shells and discard 8 of the shells. Arrange 3 scallops in each of the remaining shells and sit them in a roasting tin.

- Heat the butter in a saucepan and fry the shallot and garlic for 2 minutes to soften without colouring. Stir in the flour, then whisk in the wine, followed by the milk. Whisk gently until the mixture starts to bubble and thicken. Cook out the flour for 2 minutes then season to taste with salt, pepper and nutmeg.

- Spoon the sauce on top of the scallops. Mix the breadcrumbs with the cheese and sprinkle it over the top, then bake the scallops for 15 minutes or until golden brown and bubbling. Serve immediately.

**TOP TIP**
This recipe also works really well with oysters in place of the scallops.

# oasted Fig nd Goats' heese Salad

VES 2

PARATION TIME 5 MINUTES

KING TIME 5 MINUTES

REDIENTS

e figs, quartered

sp runny honey

g / 3 ½ oz / ½ cup crumbled goats' cheese

/ 1 ¾ oz / 1 cup baby spinach leaves

ces prosciutto, thinly shredded

sp basil leaves

sp smoked paprika

and pepper

## METHOD

- Preheat the oven to 180°C (160°C fan) / 350F / gas 4.

- Spread the figs out in a roasting tin and drizzle with honey. Season with salt and pepper then roast for 5 minutes.

- Toss the warm figs with the goats' cheese and spinach leaves and divide between 2 bowls.

- Scatter over the shredded ham and basil leaves and sprinkle with paprika then serve immediately.

**TOP TIP**
Try replacing the goats' cheese with feta.

# Main Meals

# Grilled Tuna Steak with Peppers

## SERVES 2
## PREPARATION TIME 5 MINUTES
## COOKING TIME 12 MINUTES

## INGREDIENTS

2 tbsp olive oil

1 red pepper, deseeded and diced

1 yellow pepper, deseeded and diced

1 green pepper, deseeded and diced

1 clove of garlic, finely chopped

1 tbsp runny honey

2 tbsp sherry vinegar

2 tuna steaks

salt and black pepper

## METHOD

- Preheat the grill to its highest setting.

- Heat the oil in a frying pan then fry the peppers for 8 minutes or until starting to soften. Add the garlic to the pan and fry for 1 more minute, then stir in the honey and vinegar and season with salt and pepper. Cook for 2 more minutes.

- Meanwhile, season the tuna steaks with salt and pepper, then grill for 2 minutes on each side or until cooked to your liking.

- Serve the steaks with the peppers on the side.

**TOP TIP**

Try replacing the tuna steaks with swordfish steaks.

# od with
# atay Sauce

ES 4

ARATION TIME 5 MINUTES

ING TIME 15 MINUTES

## EDIENTS

tions cod fillet

crunchy peanut butter

runny honey

light soy sauce

e, juiced

Chinese 5-spice powder

d rice to serve

## METHOD

- Preheat the oven to 190°C (170°C fan) / 375F / gas 5 and put the cod in a baking dish.

- Mix together the peanut butter, honey, soy sauce, lime juice and 5-spice, then pour it over the cod.

- Bake the cod for 15 minutes or until just cooked in the centre, then serve with the rice and the sauce from the dish spooned over.

**TOP TIP**

The cod can be replaced with any white fish, try pollock or coley.

# Mustard Pork Chops with Quick Peach Chutney

## METHOD

- Preheat the grill to its highest setting.

- Spread the pork chops with mustard then grill for 3 minutes on each side or until just cooked in the centre.

- Meanwhile, heat the oil in a saucepan and fry the onion, ginger and chilli for 5 minutes. Stir in the peaches, pepper, honey and vinegar then simmer for 5 minutes.

- Serve the chops with the warm chutney on the side and garnish with coriander.

**SERVES 4**

**PREPARATION TIME 8 MINUTES**

**COOKING TIME 12 MINUTES**

## INGREDIENTS

4 small pork chops

4 tbsp grain mustard

2 tbsp olive oil

1 onion, finely chopped

1 tsp fresh root ginger, finely chopped

1 red chilli (chili), finely chopped

2 peaches, peeled, stoned and diced

100 g / 3 ½ oz / ½ cup roasted red peppers in oil, drained and chopped

2 tbsp runny honey

2 tbsp rice wine vinegar

coriander (cilantro) to garnish

**TOP TIP**
The chutney makes a great condiment for duck breast too.

# uote with omatoes nd Prosciutto

VES 4

PARATION TIME 5 MINUTES

KING TIME 12 MINUTES

REDIENTS

g / 3 ½ oz / ⅔ cup cherry tomatoes

g / 14 oz / 4 cups dried ruote pasta

g / 3 ½ oz / ⅔ cup frozen peas, defrosted

ces prosciutto, chopped

sp Parmesan, grated

ndful of mint leaves

sp extra virgin olive oil

and black pepper

## METHOD

- Preheat the oven to 190°C (170°C fan) / 375F / gas 5. Roast the tomatoes whole for 10 minutes.

- Cook the pasta in boiling, salted water according to the packet instructions or until al dente, 2 minutes before the end of the cooking time, add the peas. Drain well, then toss with the roasted tomatoes and prosciutto.

- Divide between 4 warm bowls and top with the Parmesan and mint before dressing with olive oil, salt and pepper.

**TOP TIP**
You can also make this recipe with smoked salmon in place of the prosciutto.

# Steak and Potato Wedges

## SERVES 2
## PREPARATION TIME 8 MINUTES
## COOKING TIME 15 MINUTES

## INGREDIENTS

sunflower oil for deep-frying

4 medium potatoes, cut into wedges

2 T-bone steaks

2 tbsp butter, softened

1 clove of garlic, crushed

1 tbsp flat leaf parsley, finely chopped

salad leaves to serve

salt and black pepper

## METHOD

- Preheat the grill to its highest setting and heat the oil in a deep fat fryer, according to the manufacturer's instructions, to a temperature of 130°C

- Lower the wedges in the fryer basket and cook for 10 minutes so that they cook all the way through but don't brow

- Pull up the fryer basket and increase th fryer temperature to 190°C. When the oil has come up to temperature, lower the fryer basket and cook the wedges f or 5 minutes or until crisp and golden brown.

- While the wedges are cooking, season the steaks with salt and pepper and grill for 4 minutes on each side or until cooked to your liking. Leave to rest somewhere warm while you finish the wedges.

- Mix the butter with the garlic and parsley, then shape into 2 butter pats.

- Top each steak with a garlic butter pat and serve with the wedges and salad leaves.

**TOP TIP**

Try mashing 25 g of blue cheese into the butter.

# Spaghetti a la Carbonara

**SERVES 2**

**PREPARATION TIME 5 MINUTES**

**COOKING TIME 12 MINUTES**

## INGREDIENTS

200 g / 7 oz / 2 cups dried spaghetti

thick rashers pancetta, diced

2 tbsp olive oil

clove of garlic, crushed

large egg

50 g / 1 ¾ oz / ½ cup Parmesan, finely grated

Salt and black pepper

## METHOD

- Bring a large pan of salted water to the boil and cook the spaghetti according to the packet instructions or until al dente.

- While the pasta is cooking, fry the pancetta in the oil for 4 minutes or until golden brown. Add the garlic and cook for 2 more minutes then turn off the heat.

- Beat the egg and stir in half the grated Parmesan with a good grind of black pepper.

- When the spaghetti is ready, reserve a ladleful of the cooking water and drain the rest. Tip the spaghetti into the bacon pan and pour in the egg mixture. Mix it all together, adding enough of the cooking water to make a thick shiny sauce that clings to the pasta.

- Divide between 2 warm bowls and sprinkle over the rest of the Parmesan and some more black pepper.

**TOP TIP**

Stir a big handful of chopped parsley through the pasta.

# Lemon and Herb Pork Steaks

**SERVES 4**

**PREPARATION TIME 2 MINUTES**

**COOKING TIME 10 MINUTES**

## INGREDIENTS

4 thick pork steaks

2 tbsp olive oil

a small knob of butter

1 tsp rosemary, chopped

4 sprigs oregano, chopped

1 lemon, halved

salad leaves to serve

salt and black pepper

## METHOD

- Season the steaks liberally with salt and pepper.

- Heat the oil in a large frying pan, then add the steaks and cook for 3 minutes, turn them over and cook for 3 more minutes or until just cooked in the centre.

- Transfer the steaks to 4 warm plates. Add the butter and herbs to the pan and swirl until the butter melts.

- Squeeze in the lemon juice, then spoon the pan juices over the steaks and serve immediately with salad leaves.

**TOP TIP**

Try replacing the lemon with orange for a sweeter flavour.

# esto-stuffed ork

VES 4

PARATION TIME 15 MINUTES

KING TIME 8 MINUTES

## REDIENTS

ck pork steaks

sp pesto

sp pine nuts, roughly chopped

/ 1 oz / ¼ cup Parmesan shavings

es prosciutto, chopped

in dauphinoise to serve

## METHOD

- Preheat the grill to its highest setting.

- Cut a deep pocket into the side of each pork steak with a sharp knife. Mix the pesto with the pine nuts and Parmesan and stuff the mixture into the pockets.

- Grill the pork steaks for 4 minutes on each side or until golden brown and cooked through.

- Transfer the steaks to 4 warm plates and sprinkle over the prosciutto then serve with gratin dauphinoise.

**TOP TIP**

Try using this stuffing with chicken too.

# Tagliatelle with Prosciutto and Tomatoes

## METHOD

- Cook the tagliatelle in boiling, salted water according to the packet instructions or until al dente. Drain well.

- Return the pasta to the saucepan and toss with the rest of the ingredients, then divide between 4 warm plates and serve immediately.

**SERVES 4**

**PREPARATION TIME 5 MINUTES**

**COOKING TIME 12 MINUTES**

## INGREDIENTS

400 g / 14 oz / 4 cups dried tagliatelle
6 slices prosciutto, chopped
100 g / 3 ½ oz / ⅔ cup cherry tomatoes, quartered
a handful of rocket (arugula)
a handful of basil leaves
4 tbsp extra virgin olive oil
sea salt and black pepper

**TOP TIP**
Top the pasta with a little freshly grated lemon zest for extra zing.

# Salmon with Chorizo and Aubergine

SERVES 4

PREPARATION TIME 10 MINUTES

COOKING TIME 15 MINUTES

## INGREDIENTS

portions of salmon fillet

g / 8 oz / 1 ½ cups chorizo ring, sliced

all aubergines (eggplants), sliced
ngthways

p olive oil

mon, juiced

p flat leaf parsley, chopped

p smoked paprika

## METHOD

- Preheat the oven to 190°C (170°C fan) / 375F / gas 5.

- Spread out the salmon portions in a single layer in a roasting tin and arrange the chorizo slices on top to look like scales. Bake the salmon for 15 minutes or until the fish has just turned opaque in the centre.

- Meanwhile, brush the aubergine slices with half of the oil and griddle for 5 minutes on each side or until softened and nicely marked. Transfer to a shallow bowl. Mix the rest of the oil with the lemon juice and parsley and drizzle it over the aubergine.

- Divide the salmon between 4 warm plates and sprinkle with paprika. Spoon the aubergine slices alongside with their dressing.

**TOP TIP**
This recipe also works really well with cod in place of the salmon.

# Bunless Egg and Onion Burgers

## SERVES 2
## PREPARATION TIME 10 MINUTES
## COOKING TIME 16 MINUTES

## INGREDIENTS

450 g / 1 lb / 2 cups beef mince

2 tbsp double (heavy) cream

1 tsp Dijon mustard

4 tbsp sunflower oil

1 large onion, sliced into rings

4 large eggs

½ tsp paprika

mixed salad leaves and barbecue sauce,
   to serve

salt and black pepper

## METHOD

- Mix the beef with the cream and mustard and season generously with salt and pepper, then knead lightly until sticky. Divide the mixture into four and press each piece into a ring mould to get an even shape.

- Heat half of the oil in a frying pan then fry the burgers for 8 minutes, turning every 2 minutes. Wrap the burgers in a double layer of foil and leave them to rest while you cook the eggs and onions.

- Add another tablespoon of oil to the pan and fry the onion rings for 2 minutes on each side or until they're just starting to brown and soften.

- Add the final tablespoon of oil to the pan and put the burger ring moulds in to heat. Crack and egg into each one and sprinkle the tops with paprika. Cook for 4 minutes or until the whites are set, but the yolks are still a little runny.

- Top the burgers with the onion and eggs and serve with the salad leaves and barbecue sauce on the side.

**TOP TIP**
Add a few slices of crispy bacon for extra decadence.

# Macaroni with Courgette and Smoked Salmon

**SERVES 4**

**PREPARATION TIME 5 MINUTES**

**COOKING TIME 20 MINUTES**

## INGREDIENTS

400 g / 14 oz / 3 cups dried elbow macaroni

2 courgettes (zucchinis), halved and thinly sliced

1 tbsp Dijon mustard

4 tbsp crème fraiche

4 slices smoked salmon, chopped

50 g / 1 ¾ oz / ½ cup Emmental, grated

salt

## METHOD

- Preheat the oven to 190°C (170°C fan) / 375F / gas 5.

- Cook the macaroni in boiling, salted water for 5 minutes. Add the courgettes and cook for 3 more minutes or until the macaroni is al dente. Drain well.

- Stir the mustard into the crème fraiche, then stir it into the macaroni and courgettes with the smoked salmon.

- Spoon the pasta mixture into a greased baking dish and sprinkle the top with cheese. Bake the macaroni for 10 minutes or until the top is golden brown.

**TOP TIP**

Try prosciutto instead of the smoked salmon.

# Swordfish with Tomato and Passion Fruit Salsa

## METHOD

- Preheat the grill to its highest setting.

- Season the swordfish with salt, then grill for 2 minutes on each side or until cooked to your liking.

- Meanwhile, stir the onion, tomato, garlic and coriander together. Pass the passion fruit pulp through a sieve to remove the seeds, then stir the juice into salsa. Season to taste with salt and pepper.

- Spoon the salsa over the swordfish and serve immediately.

**SERVES 2**

**PREPARATION TIME 10 MINUTES**

**COOKING TIME 4 MINUTES**

## INGREDIENTS

2 swordfish steaks

1 small onion, finely chopped

4 medium tomatoes, deseeded and finely diced

½ clove of garlic, crushed

2 tbsp coriander (cilantro) leaves, finely chopped

2 passion fruit, halved

salt and black pepper

**TOP TIP**
Try replacing the tomatoes with mango for a totally tropical taste.

# urkey Burgers

VES 4

**PARATION TIME 20 MINUTES**

**KING TIME 8 MINUTES**

## REDIENTS

g / 1 lb / 2 cups turkey breast, cubed
ove of garlic, crushed
sp lemon zest, finely grated
/ 1 oz / ¼ cup Parmesan, finely grated
sp olive oil
matoes, diced
nall onion, finely chopped
sp flat leaf parsley, chopped
esame buns, split in half
sp tomato ketchup
and black pepper

## METHOD

- Put the turkey, garlic, lemon zest and Parmesan in a food processor and pulse until finely chopped and evenly mixed. Shape the mixture into 4 patties and chill in the freezer for 15 minutes to firm up.

- Meanwhile, heat a cast iron griddle pan on the hob until smoking hot. Brush the burgers with oil then griddle for 4 minutes on each side or until nicely marked and cooked through.

- While the burgers are cooking, mix the tomato, onion and parsley together and season with salt and pepper to make a salsa.

- Spread the bottom half of the buns with ketchup, then position the burgers on top and spoon over the salsa. Sit the bun tops on top and serve immediately.

**TOP TIP**
Try using chicken instead of turkey and top the burgers with crispy bacon.

# Spaghetti with Courgette and Haricot Beans

## METHOD

- Cook the spaghetti in boiling salted water according to the packet instructions or until al dente. Drain well.

- Meanwhile, heat the oil in a sauté pan and fry the courgettes for 8 minutes or until starting to soften. Stir in the haricot beans and warm through, then toss with the spaghetti and goats' cheese.

- Divide between 4 warm bowls and garnish with oregano and freshly ground black pepper.

**SERVES 4**

**PREPARATION TIME 5 MINUTES**

**COOKING TIME 12 MINUTES**

## INGREDIENTS

400 g / 14 oz / 3 ½ cups dried spaghetti

4 tbsp olive oil

2 courgettes (zucchinis), sliced

400 g / 14 oz / 1 ½ cups canned haricot beans, drained

100 g / 3 ½ oz / ½ cup crumbled goats' cheese

oregano sprigs to garnish

salt and black pepper

**TOP TIP**
This recipe also works really well with chickpeas instead of haricot beans.

# rib-eye with tomatoes

SERVES 1

PREPARATION TIME 10 MINUTES

COOKING TIME 6 MINUTES

INGREDIENTS

large rib-eye steak

tsp olive oil

sprig of rosemary

clove of garlic, halved

cherry tomatoes, halved

salt and black pepper

## METHOD

- Put a frying pan over a high heat and season the steak liberally with salt and pepper.

- Drizzle the oil over the base of the pan then lower in the steak and add the rosemary, garlic and tomatoes, cut side down, next to it.

- Cook without disturbing for 3 minutes, then turn everything over and cook for another 3 minutes. If you prefer your steak well-done, cook it for another 2–3 minutes on each side.

- Wrap the steak in a double layer of foil and leave to rest for 5 minutes, then serve with the tomatoes.

## TOP TIP

Try replacing the tomatoes with baby button mushrooms.

# Rigatoni with Tomatoes and Feta

**SERVES 2**

**PREPARATION TIME 5 MINUTES**

**COOKING TIME 12 MINUTES**

## INGREDIENTS

200 g / 7 oz / 2 cups dried rigatoni

100 g / 3 ½ oz / ⅔ cup feta, crumbled

100 g / 3 ½ oz / ⅔ cup cherry tomatoes, halved

4 slices cooked ham, chopped

a handful of basil leaves

4 tbsp olive oil

2 tbsp Parmesan, finely grated

salt and black pepper

## METHOD

- Cook the rigatoni in boiling, salted water according to the packet instructions or until al dente.

- Drain well then toss with the feta, tomatoes, ham and basil leaves.

- Divide between 2 warm bowls and dress with the olive oil, then sprinkle with Parmesan and black pepper.

**TOP TIP**

Try replacing the feta with crumbled Stilton.

# Mushroom Fricassee with Eggs

**SERVES 2**

**PREPARATION TIME 10 MINUTES**

**COOKING TIME 20 MINUTES**

## INGREDIENTS

sp olive oil

sp butter

g / 5 ½ oz / 2 cups button mushrooms, alved

shers streaky bacon, halved

ove of garlic, crushed

nl / 1 ¾ oz / ¼ cup dry white wine

ml / 3 ½ fl. oz / ½ cup double (heavy) ream, plus extra to garnish

ge eggs

sp Parmesan, finely grated

leaf parsley to garnish

## METHOD

- Preheat the oven to 180°C (160°C fan) / 350F / gas 4.

- Heat the oil and butter in a sauté pan and fry the mushrooms and bacon for 5 minutes, stirring occasionally. Stir in the garlic and cook for 1 more minute, then pour in the wine and reduce by half. Stir in the cream and simmer for 2 minutes.

- Scrape the mixture into an enamel baking dish and break in the eggs. Transfer the dish to the oven and bake for 10 minutes or until the egg whites are just set.

- Sprinkle over the Parmesan and garnish with parsley then serve immediately.

**TOP TIP**

Try replacing the bacon with chorizo for a spicy kick.

# Artichoke and Feta Pasta Salad

## METHOD

- Cook the rigatoni in boiling, salted water according to the packet instructions or until al dente. Drain well, then plunge into iced water to quickly cool it to room temperature. Drain again.

- Toss the pasta with the spinach, artichokes, olives, feta and cherry tomatoes.

- Whisk the oil with the lemon juice, garlic and chilli flakes and season generously with salt and pepper. Toss the dressing with the salad, then divide between 4 bowls and serve immediately.

**SERVES 4**

**PREPARATION TIME 10 MINUTES**

**COOKING TIME 12 MINUTES**

## INGREDIENTS

300 g / 11 oz / 3 cups dried rigatoni

100 g / 3 ½ oz / 3 cups baby leaf spinach

300 g / 10 ½ oz / 1 ½ cups artichokes in oil, drained and quartered

75 g / 2 ½ oz / ½ cup black olives

100 g / 3 ½ oz / ⅔ cup feta, crumbled

150 g / 5 ½ oz / 1 cup cherry tomatoes, halved

4 tbsp olive oil

1 lemon, juiced

½ clove of garlic, crushed

½ tsp dried chilli (chili) flakes

salt and black pepper

**TOP TIP**

Try replacing the olives with capers.

# Lamb Chops with Cheese, Tomato and Bacon

SERVES 2

PREPARATION TIME 5 MINUTES

COOKING TIME 20 MINUTES

## INGREDIENTS

lamb chops, French trimmed

slices Brie

tomato, sliced

rashers streaky bacon

lemon, cut into wedges

## METHOD

- Preheat the oven to 200°C (180°C fan) / 400F / gas 6.

- Top each lamb chop with a slice of Brie and a slice of tomato, then wrap them tightly in the bacon. Transfer the chops to a roasting tin and surround with the lemon wedges then roast for 20 minutes.

- Serve the chops with the roasted lemon wedges for squeezing over.

**TOP TIP**

This recipe also works really well with pork chops.

# Blackened Duck Breast with Cherry Tomatoes

**SERVES 2**

**PREPARATION TIME 20 MINUTES**

**COOKING TIME 10 MINUTES**

## INGREDIENTS

2 tbsp runny honey

1 tsp Dijon mustard

½ tbsp Worcestershire sauce

½ tsp dried rosemary

2 duck breasts

200 g / 7 oz / 1 ⅓ cups cherry tomatoes on the vine

## METHOD

- Preheat the oven to 220°C (200°C fan) / 425F / gas 7.

- Mix the honey, mustard, Worcestershire sauce and rosemary together and massage it into the duck breasts. Leave to marinate for 10 minutes.

- Transfer the duck breasts to a roasting tin and lay the tomato vines next to them, then roast for 10 minutes or until the duck is deeply caramelised on the outside, but still pink in the middle.

- Leave the duck to rest for 5 minutes then slice and serve with the tomatoes.

**TOP TIP**
For extra depth of flavour, marinade the duck for up to 4 hours before cooking.

# Stuffed Chicken Breast with Root Vegetables

SERVES 4

PREPARATION TIME 2 MINUTES

COOKING TIME 28 MINUTES

## INGREDIENTS

carrots, quartered

parsnips, cut into thin wedges

tbsp olive oil

tbsp butter

shallot, finely chopped

garlic clove, crushed

g / 1 oz / ⅓ cup fresh breadcrumbs

g / 1 ¾ oz / ⅓ cup pine nuts, finely chopped

tbsp basil leaves, finely chopped

tbsp Parmesan, finely grated

chicken breasts, skin-on

Salt and black pepper

## METHOD

- Preheat the oven to 220°C (200°C fan) / 430F / gas 7. Put the carrots and parsnips in a roasting tin and drizzle with olive oil, then roast in the oven for 10 minutes.

- Meanwhile, heat the butter in a frying pan and fry the shallot and garlic for 4 minutes or until softened but not coloured. Take the pan off the heat and stir in the breadcrumbs, pine nuts, basil and Parmesan, then season with salt and pepper.

- Cut a deep pocket into the side of each chicken breast and fill with the stuffing mixture.

- Transfer the chicken to the roasting tin, reduce the temperature to 190°C (170°C fan) / 375F / gas 5 and cook for a further 18 minutes or until the chicken is cooked through and the vegetables are tender.

- Serve the chicken immediately with the root vegetables on the side.

**TOP TIP**

Use chicken thigh quarters instead of the breasts. Make a pocket in the flesh.

# Cep-stuffed Veal Steaks

**SERVES 4**

**PREPARATION TIME 15 MINUTES**

**COOKING TIME 15 MINUTES**

## INGREDIENTS

4 thick veal steaks

2 tbsp butter

150 g / 5 ½ oz / 2 cups ceps, sliced

1 clove of garlic, crushed

2 tbsp flat leaf parsley, chopped

2 tbsp crème fraiche

salt and black pepper

## METHOD

- Preheat the grill to its highest setting and cut a deep pocket into the side of each veal steak with a sharp knife.

- Heat the butter in a frying pan then fry the ceps for 5 minutes, turning occasionally. Remove from the pan with a slotted spoon and reserve half of them as a garnish. Slice the rest into matchsticks.

- Add the garlic and parsley to the frying pan and fry for 1 minute, then stir in the crème fraiche and cep matchsticks.

- Stuff the cep mixture into the veal pockets, season and then grill the steaks for 3 minutes on each side or until cooked to your liking.

- Transfer the steaks to 4 warm plates and garnish with the reserved ceps.

**TOP TIP**

This stuffing also works really well with guinea fowl breasts.

# esame Meatball asta

VES 4

PARATION TIME 15 MINUTES

KING TIME 15 MINUTES

## REDIENTS

g / 8 oz / 1 cup minced lamb
g / 8 oz / 1 cup sausagemeat
/ 2 oz / ⅔ cup fresh white breadcrumbs
sp hummus
sp flat leaf parsley, finely chopped
sp sesame seeds
sp olive oil
g / 14 oz / 4 cups dried fusilli
erry tomatoes, quartered
/ 1 ¾ oz / ½ cup Parmesan, finely grated
l leaves to garnish
and black pepper

## METHOD

- Knead the lamb mince, sausagemeat, breadcrumbs, hummus and parsley together and season with salt and pepper. Shape the mixture into meatballs and roll in the sesame seeds to coat.

- Heat half of the oil in a frying pan and fry the meatballs for 15 minutes or until cooked through, turning occasionally.

- Meanwhile, boil the pasta in salted water according to the packet instructions or until al dente.

- Drain the pasta then toss it with the meatballs and tomatoes and dress with the rest of the oil. Divide between 4 warm bowls and sprinkle generously with Parmesan. Garnish with basil leaves.

**TOP TIP**
Try rolling half of the meatballs in poppy seeds for a pretty presentation.

# Veal Piccata

## METHOD

- Put a frying pan over a high heat. Season the veal liberally with salt and pepper, then dust it with flour.

- Add the olive oil and half the butter to the pan. When the butter stops sizzling, lower in the escalopes. Cook without disturbing for 3 minutes, then turn them over and cook for another 3 minutes. Remove the veal from the pan and wrap in a double layer of foil to rest.

- Add the wine and a squeeze of lemon to the pan and reduce until only 2 tbsp of liquid remains. Whisk in the rest of the butter until foamy.

- Serve the veal with potato batons and cherry tomatoes on the side and spoon over the foaming pan juices.

## SERVES 2
## PREPARATION TIME 5 MINUTES
## COOKING TIME 10 MINUTES

## INGREDIENTS

2 veal escalopes

2 tbsp plain (all purpose) flour

1 tbsp olive oil

2 tbsp butter

50 ml / 1 ¾ fl. oz / ¼ cup dry white wine

½ lemon

boiled potato batons and halved cherry tomatoes to serve

salt and black pepper

**TOP TIP**

This recipe also works well with chicken escallops.

# Chickpea and Tomato Salad

SERVES 2

PREPARATION TIME 5 MINUTES

## INGREDIENTS

400 g / 14 oz / 1 ½ cups canned chickpeas (garbanzo beans), drained

1 cucumber, peeled and diced

150 g / 5 ½ oz / 1 cup cherry tomatoes, halved

3 tbsp extra virgin olive oil

1 tbsp lemon juice

pinch of ground cumin

salt

## METHOD

- Toss the chickpeas with the cucumber and tomatoes and divide between 2 bowls.

- Whisk the oil and lemon juice together with the cumin and a pinch of salt until emulsified, then drizzle it over the salads and serve immediately.

**TOP TIP**

This also tastes great with butterbeans in place of the chickpeas.

# Vegetable Tart

## METHOD

- Preheat the oven to 190°C (170°C fan) / 375F / gas 5.

- Spoon the hummus into the tart case and arrange the vegetables and chickpeas on top.

- Transfer the tart to the oven and bake for 20 minutes or until the vegetables are tender and golden brown on top.

## SERVES 4

## PREPARATION TIME 5 MINUTES

## COOKING TIME 20 MINUTES

## INGREDIENTS

200 g / 7 oz / ¾ cup hummus

1 savory shortcrust pastry case

4 asparagus spears

1 red onion, sliced

1 courgette (zucchini), sliced

½ red pepper, deseeded and sliced

100 g / 3 ½ oz / ¾ cup preserved artichokes in brine, drained and sliced

4 button mushrooms, sliced

2 tbsp canned chickpeas, drained

**TOP TIP**
Crack an egg into the centre of the tart before baking for a deliciously soft centre.

# Roast Guinea Fowl Breast with Asparagus

SERVES 4

PREPARATION TIME 5 MINUTES

COOKING TIME 25 MINUTES

## INGREDIENTS

guinea fowl supremes

225 g / 8 oz / 1 cup white asparagus spears, trimmed

225 g / 8 oz / 1 cup green asparagus spears, trimmed

lemon, juiced and zest finely grated

tbsp runny honey

tbsp tarragon, finely chopped

150 g / 5 ½ oz / ⅔ cup cold-smoked haddock loin

salad leaves to serve

salt and pepper

## METHOD

- Preheat the oven to 180°C (160°C fan) / 350F / gas 4.

- Season the guinea fowl supremes well with salt and pepper, then roast them for 25 minutes or until the juices run clear when you pierce the thickest part with a skewer.

- Meanwhile, steam the asparagus for 6 minutes or until tender.

- Mix the lemon juice and zest with the honey and tarragon to make a dressing.

- Roughly chop the haddock with a sharp knife.

- Serve the guinea fowl with the steamed asparagus on the side. Drizzle over the lemon dressing and top each plate with a few slices of smoked haddock. Garnish with salad leaves.

**TOP TIP**
Replace the smoked haddock with chunks of pan-fried chorizo.

# Penne with Courgette and Lardons

**SERVES 4**

**PREPARATION TIME 5 MINUTES**

**COOKING TIME 12 MINUTES**

## INGREDIENTS

400 g / 14 oz / 3 cups dried penne pasta

4 tbsp olive oil

100 g / 2 ⅓ oz / ½ cup lardons

1 large courgette (zucchini), cut into batons

thyme sprigs to garnish

sea salt

## METHOD

- Cook the penne in boiling, salted water according to the packet instructions or until al dente. Drain well.

- While the pasta is cooking, heat the oil in a frying pan and fry the lardons and courgette batons for 6 minutes or until golden brown.

- Toss the pasta with the lardons and courgettes, then divide between 4 warm bowls and garnish with thyme.

**TOP TIP**

Try replacing the courgette with sugar snap peas.

# egetable kewers

**ES 4**

**PARATION TIME 20 MINUTES**

**KING TIME 8 MINUTES**

**REDIENTS**

sp olive oil

sp cider vinegar

p dried herbes de Provence

urgette (zucchini), cut into chunks

herry tomatoes, halved

utton mushrooms, halved

nnel bulb, cut into chunks

and black pepper

## METHOD

- Mix the oil with the vinegar, herbs and a pinch of salt and pepper. Pour the mixture over the vegetables and leave to marinate for 15 minutes.

- Meanwhile, soak 12 wooden skewers in a bowl of cold water.

- Preheat the grill to its highest setting. Thread the vegetables onto the skewers.

- Cook the kebabs under the grill for 8 minutes, turning occasionally, or until the vegetables are tender and lightly toasted round the edges.

**TOP TIP**

Try adding chunks of halloumi to the skewers for a great combination of textures.

# Pork and Grapefruit Salad

**SERVES 4**

**PREPARATION TIME 15 MINUTES**

**COOKING TIME 5 MINUTES**

## INGREDIENTS

2 ruby grapefruit

2 tbsp olive oil

1 pork fillet, sliced

2 handfuls of rocket (arugula)

4 crostini toasts

2 tbsp pine nuts

salt and black pepper

## METHOD

- Slice the top and bottom off the grapefruit. Slice away the peel then cut out each individual segment, leaving the white pith behind like the pages of a book and collecting any juices in a bowl. Discard the pith.

- Heat the oil in a large frying pan. Season the pieces of pork fillet with salt and pepper, then fry them for 1 minute on each side or until just cooked through. Remove the pork from the pan and deglaze with the collected grapefruit juices.

- Toss the pork with the rocket and grapefruit segments and divide between 4 plates. Break the crostini into pieces and scatter over the top with the pine nuts. Dress the salads with the pan juices and serve immediately.

**TOP TIP**
Try using chicken livers instead of the pork for an economical treat.

# Desserts

# Maraschino Cherry Clafoutis

## SERVES 6
## PREPARATION TIME 5 MINUTES
## COOKING TIME 25 MINUTES

## INGREDIENTS

75 g / 2 ½ oz / ⅓ cup butter

75 g / 2 ½ oz / ⅓ cup caster (superfine) sugar

300 ml / 10 ½ fl. oz / 1 ¼ cups whole milk

2 large eggs

50 g / 1 ¾ oz / ⅓ cup plain (all purpose) flour

2 tbsp ground almonds

200 g / 7 oz / 1 ⅓ cups maraschino cherries,
    drained with stalks intact

pinch of salt

## METHOD

- Preheat the oven to 190°C (170°C fan) / 375F / gas 5.

- Melt the butter in a saucepan and cook over a low heat until it starts to smell nutty. Brush a little of the butter around the inside of a 20 cm (8 in) diameter quiche dish then add a spoonful of caster sugar and shake to coat.

- Whisk together the milk and eggs with the rest of the butter. Sift the flour into a mixing bowl with a pinch of salt and stir in the ground almonds and the rest of the sugar.

- Make a well in the middle of the dry ingredients and gradually whisk in the liquid, incorporating all the flour from round the outside until you have a lump-free batter.

- Arrange the cherries in the prepared baking dish, pour over the batter and transfer to the oven immediately. Bake the clafoutis for 20–25 minutes or until a skewer inserted in the centre comes out clean.

**TOP TIP**
Try sprinkling the clafoutis with flaked almonds before baking for added crunch.

# Speedy Summer Fruit Trifle

## SERVES 8

### PREPARATION TIME 10 MINUTES

## INGREDIENTS

300 g / 10 ½ oz / 2 cups lemon Madeira cake, sliced

4 tbsp limoncello

50 g / 1 ¾ oz / ½ cup icing (confectioners') sugar

225 g / 8 oz / 1 cup Greek yoghurt

225 g / 8 oz / 1 cup mascarpone

200 g / 7 oz / 1 ⅓ cups raspberries

200 g / 7 oz / 1 ⅓ cups blueberries

## METHOD

- Lay half of the cake slices in a trifle bowl and sprinkle with half of the limoncello.

- Fold the icing sugar into the yoghurt and mascarpone, then spoon half of it over the cake.

- Top with half of the berries, then cover with the rest of the cake and limoncello. Spoon the rest of the yoghurt mixture on top and scatter over the rest of the berries.

- Serve straight away or leave for 20 minutes for the flavours to infuse.

**TOP TIP**

Add the grated zest of an orange and lemon to the mascarpone mixture.

# DESSERTS

# Sweet Bagel Sandwich

**SERVES 1**

**PREPARATION TIME 3 MINUTES**

**COOKING TIME 2 MINUTES**

## INGREDIENTS

1 sugar-topped bagel, split in half

1 tbsp lemon curd

1 large strawberry, sliced

4 raspberries

½ tsp lime zest, finely grated

a small sprig of mint

## METHOD

- Toast the bagel, then spread the bottom half with lemon curd.

- Arrange the strawberry slices and raspberries on top, then sprinkle with lime zest and garnish with mint. Serve immediately.

**TOP TIP**
Top the fruit with a spoonful of whipped cream for extra decadence.

# Speedy Raspberry and Almond Rice Puddings

**SERVES 6**

**PREPARATION TIME 15 MINUTES**

**COOKING TIME 10 MINUTES**

## INGREDIENTS

g / 4 oz / ½ cup short grain rice

g / 2 ½ oz / ¼ cup runny honey

litres / 2 pints / 4 ½ cups almond milk

g / 9 oz / 1 ⅔ cups raspberries

g / 1 oz / ⅓ cup flaked (slivered) almonds

## METHOD

- Preheat the oven to 140°C (120°C fan) / 275F / gas 1.

- Stir the rice and honey into the almond milk in a microwavable bowl, then cover with cling film and pierce the top.

- Cook on high for 5 minutes, then stir well and cook for another 5 minutes or until all the milk has been absorbed and the rice is tender. Leave to stand for 5 minutes.

- Crush half of the raspberries with a fork, then stir the puree into the rice with the whole berries, reserving a few for decoration.

- Divide the rice pudding between 6 glasses and sprinkle the almonds and reserved raspberries over the top.

**TOP TIP**

The rice puddings are also delicious served chilled if you make them in advance.

# Blackberry and Apple Compote with Meringue Topping

**SERVES 6**

**PREPARATION TIME 15 MINUTES**

**COOKING TIME 15 MINUTES**

### INGREDIENTS

2 Bramley apples, peeled, cored and chopped

200 g / 7 oz / 1 ⅓ cups blackberries

50 g / 1 ¾ oz / ¼ cup granulated sugar

4 large egg whites

110 g / 4 oz / 1 cup caster (superfine) sugar

## METHOD

- Put the apples, blackberries and granulated sugar in a saucepan with a splash of water. Cover the pan and cook over a medium heat for 10 minutes or until the fruit has broken down into a thick compote, stirring occasionally. Spoon the compote into 6 glasses.

- Whisk the egg whites until stiff, then gradually whisk in half the sugar until the mixture is very shiny. Fold in the remaining sugar with a large metal spoon.

- Spoon the meringue into a piping bag fitted with a large star nozzle and pipe a swirl on top of the compote in each glass.

- Toast the tops under a hot grill for 3–4 minutes or until golden brown. Serve immediately.

**TOP TIP**

Crumble some sponge cake into the bottom of each glass first.

# Chocolate and Hazelnut Brownies

**MAKES 16**

**PREPARATION TIME 5 MINUTES**

**COOKING TIME 25 MINUTES**

## INGREDIENTS

- 00 g / 4 oz / ½ cup dark chocolate (minimum 70% cocoa solids), chopped
- g / 3 oz / ¾ cup unsweetened cocoa powder, sifted
- 5 g / 8 oz / 1 cup butter
- 0 g / 1 lb / 2 ½ cups light brown sugar
- arge eggs
- 0 g / 4 oz / 1 cup self-raising flour
- g / 2 ½ oz / ½ cup toasted hazelnuts (cob nuts), chopped

## METHOD

- Preheat the oven to 160°C (140°C fan) / 325F / gas 3 and oil and line a 20 cm x 20 cm (8 in x 8 in) square cake tin.

- Melt the chocolate, cocoa and butter together in a saucepan, then leave to cool a little.

- Whisk the sugar and eggs together with an electric whisk for 3 minutes or until very light and creamy.

- Pour in the chocolate mixture and sift over the flour. Reserve 1 tbsp of the nuts to decorate and fold the rest into the brownie batter.

- Scrape into the tin and bake for 25 minutes or until the outside is set, but the centre is still quite soft.

- Leave the brownie to cool completely before cutting into 12 squares and sprinkling with the reserved hazelnuts.

**TOP TIP**

Try adding the grated zest of an orange when you melt the butter.

# Ginger Nuts

## MAKES 36
## PREPARATION TIME 10 MINUTES
## COOKING TIME 15 MINUTES

### INGREDIENTS

75 g / 2 ½ oz / ⅓ cup butter, softened
100 g / 3 ½ oz / ⅓ cup golden syrup
225 g / 8 oz / 1 ½ cups self-raising flour
100 g / 3 ½ oz / ½ cup caster (superfine) sugar
2 tsp ground ginger
1 large egg, beaten

### METHOD

- Preheat the oven to 180°C (160°C fan) / 355F / gas 4 and line 2 baking sheets with greaseproof paper.

- Melt the butter and golden syrup together in a saucepan. Mix the flour, sugar and ground ginger together then stir in the melted butter mixture and the beaten egg.

- Use a teaspoon to portion the mixture onto the baking trays, leaving plenty of room for the biscuits to spread.

- Bake for 15 minutes or until golden brown. Transfer the biscuits to a wire rack and leave to cool and harden.

**TOP TIP**
Try replacing the ground ginger with ground cinnamon for a sweet and spicy treat.

# oasted
# ineapple

**VES 4**

**PARATION TIME 5 MINUTES**

**KING TIME 25 MINUTES**

## REDIENTS

neapple, peeled and cored

g / 7 oz / ¾ cup caster (superfine) sugar

nnamon stick

rdamom pods

ar anise

ece orange peel

naretti biscuits, crushed

oops vanilla ice cream

sp crème fraiche

mel shards, mint leaves and plum slices

o garnish

## METHOD

- Preheat the oven to 200°C (180°C fan) / 400F / gas 6 and cut the pineapple into even-sized batons.

- Put the sugar, spices and orange peel in a saucepan with 300 ml / ½ pint / 1 ¼ cups of water and stir over a medium heat to dissolve the sugar. Once the sugar has dissolved, stop stirring and let it boil for 8 minutes or until thick and syrupy. Strain it into a jug to remove the spices.

- Arrange the pineapple in a roasting tin in a single layer and pour over three quarters of the spiced syrup. Roast the pineapple for 15 minutes, turning the pieces over halfway through.

- Arrange the pineapple batons on 4 plates. Add a spoonful of crushed amaretti to each plate and top with a scoop of ice cream.

- Spoon the crème fraiche around the plate, then garnish with caramel shards, mint leaves and plum slices.

**TOP TIP**
Serve with coconut ice cream and a drizzle of chocolate sauce.

# Apple and Amaretti Verrines

## SERVES 4

## PREPARATION TIME 5 MINUTES

## INGREDIENTS

50 g / 1 ¾ oz / ½ cup icing (confectioners')
     sugar, sieved

450 g / 1 lb / 2 cups Greek yoghurt

50 g / 1 ¾ oz / ½ cup apple compote

100 g / 3 ½ oz / 2 cups amaretti biscuits,
     crushed

4 tbsp Amaretto liqueur

## METHOD

- Stir the icing sugar into the yoghurt.

- Fold the apple compote into the crushed biscuits and divide half of the mixture between 4 glasses. Drizzle with half of the liqueur.

- Spoon over half of the yoghurt, then top with the rest of the compote mixture and drizzle with the rest of the liqueur.

- Top with the rest of the yoghurt and serve immediately.

**TOP TIP**
Try replacing the apple with peaches when they're in season.

# Chocolate and Walnut Brownie Cake

SERVES 8

PREPARATION TIME 5 MINUTES

COOKING TIME 25 MINUTES

## INGREDIENTS

g / 4 oz / ½ cup dark chocolate (minimum 70% cocoa solids), chopped

g / 3 oz / ¾ cup unsweetened cocoa powder, sifted

g / 8 oz / 1 cup butter

g / 1 lb / 2 ½ cups light brown sugar

large eggs

g / 4 oz / 1 cup self-raising flour

g / 2 ½ oz / ½ cup walnuts, finely chopped

## METHOD

- Preheat the oven to 160°C (140°C fan) / 325F / gas 3 and oil and line a 23 cm (9 in) round cake tin with greaseproof paper.

- Melt the chocolate, cocoa and butter together in a saucepan, then leave to cool a little.

- Whisk the sugar and eggs together with an electric whisk for 3 minutes or until very light and creamy.

- Pour in the chocolate mixture and sieve over the flour, then fold everything together with the walnuts.

- Scrape the mixture into the tin and bake for 25 minutes or until the outside is set, but the centre is still quite soft.

- Leave the brownie to cool completely before cutting into wedges and serving.

**TOP TIP**

Replace the walnuts with chopped salted peanuts for a sweet and salty taste sensation.

# Apple Tart

**SERVES 4**

**PREPARATION TIME 10 MINUTES**

**COOKING TIME 20 MINUTES**

## INGREDIENTS

400 g / 14 oz / 1 ⅓ cups ready-to-roll puff
    pastry

3 tbsp apricot jam (jelly)

2 apples, peeled, cored and sliced

## METHOD

- Preheat the oven to 220°C (200°C fan) / 425F / gas 7.

- Roll out the pastry into a long, narrow rectangle on a lightly floured surface. Transfer the pastry to a non-stick baking tray.

- Spread the top of the pastry with apricot jam, leaving a 1 cm (½ in) border around the outside. Arrange the apple slices on top in a single layer.

- Transfer the baking tray to the oven and bake for 20 minutes or until the pastry is cooked through underneath.

**TOP TIP**

This recipe is also delicious made with pears or plums.

# Raspberry and Nut Yoghurt Pots

**RVES 4**

**EPARATION TIME 5 MINUTES**

## GREDIENTS

bsp runny honey

0 g / 1 lb / 2 cups Greek yoghurt

raspberries

bsp pistachio nuts, roughly chopped

bsp pine nuts

sp balsamic vinegar

## METHOD

- Stir the honey into the yoghurt and divide between 4 glasses.

- Decorate the yoghurt with the raspberries, pistachios and pine nuts, then drizzle with balsamic vinegar.

**TOP TIP**

This recipe is also delicious made with blueberries in place of the raspberries.

# Strawberry and Raspberry Mousse

## SERVES 4

## PREPARATION TIME 30 MINUTES

## INGREDIENTS

150 g / 5 ½ oz / 1 cup strawberries, quartered

150 g / 5 ½ oz / 1 cup raspberries

4 tbsp caster (superfine) sugar

175 ml / 6 fl. oz / ⅔ cup canned evaporated milk, chilled

225 g / 8 oz / 1 cup Greek yoghurt

## METHOD

- Reserve a few of the strawberries and raspberries for decoration and put the rest in a liquidiser with the sugar. Blend until smooth, then pass the mixture through a sieve to remove the seeds.

- Whip the evaporated milk with an electric whisk for 6 minutes or until doubled in volume.

- Fold in the fruit puree and yoghurt, then spoon into 4 glasses and chill for 20 minutes.

- Top with the reserved fruit and serve immediately.

**TOP TIP**
This recipe also works really well with blueberries and blackberries.

# Marinated Summer Berries

## METHOD

- Mix all of the ingredients together and leave to marinate for 30 minutes.

- Spoon into 6 small bowls and serve immediately.

## RVES 6
## EPARATION TIME 30 MINUTES

## GREDIENTS

) g / 5 ½ oz / 1 cup strawberries, halved

) g / 5 ½ oz / 1 cup raspberries

) g / 5 ½ oz / 1 cup blackberries

) g / 5 ½ oz / 1 cup blueberries

bsp caster (superfine) sugar

bsp mint, roughly chopped

mes, juiced

**TOP TIP**

Try adding 4 tbsp of crème de cassis to the marinade.

# Apricot and Almond Puddings

## SERVES 4

### PREPARATION TIME 10 MINUTES

### COOKING TIME 20 MINUTES

## INGREDIENTS

55 g / 2 oz / ½ cup ground almonds

55 g / 2 oz / ¼ cup caster (superfine) sugar

55 g / 2 oz / ¼ cup butter, softened

1 large egg

1 tsp almond essence

4 canned apricot halves

1 tbsp granulated sugar

2 tbsp flaked (slivered) almonds

lemon thyme to garnish

## METHOD

- Preheat the oven to 200°C (180°C fan) / 400F / gas 6.

- Combine the ground almonds, sugar, butter, egg and almond essence in a bowl and whisk together for 2 minutes or until smooth.

- Spoon the mixture into 4 individual baking dishes, then top each one with an apricot half and sprinkle with granulated sugar.

- Bake the puddings for 20 minutes, then garnish with flaked almonds and lemon thyme.

**TOP TIP**

Try using canned pears in place of the apricots.

# Crepes with Chocolate Dipping Sauce

**SERVES 4**

**PREPARATION TIME 10 MINUTES**

**COOKING TIME 20 MINUTES**

### INGREDIENTS

150 g / 5 ½ oz / 1 cup plain (all purpose) flour
1 large egg
325 ml / 11 ½ fl. oz / 1 ⅓ cups whole milk
1 tbsp butter

#### THE DIPPING SAUCE

100 ml / 3 ½ fl. oz / 1 ½ cups double (heavy)cream
1 tbsp brandy
100 g / 3 ½ oz / ½ cup dark chocolate (minimum 60 % cocoa solids), chopped

## METHOD

- To make the dipping sauce, heat the cream and brandy to simmering point then pour it over the chocolate and stir to emulsify. Spoon into 4 serving bowls.

- Sieve the flour into a bowl and make a well in the centre. Break in the egg and pour in the milk then use a whisk to gradually incorporate all of the flour from round the outside.

- Melt the butter in a small frying pan then whisk it into the batter.

- Put the buttered frying pan back over a low heat. Add a small ladle of batter and swirl the pan to coat the bottom.

- When it starts to dry and curl up at the edges, turn the pancake over with a spatula and cook the other side until golden brown and cooked through.

- Repeat with the rest of the mixture then serve the crepes with the dipping sauce.

**TOP TIP**
Serve the crepes with vanilla ice cream for a great hot and cold combination.

# Marinated Strawberry and Lemon Verrines

## SERVES 4

## PREPARATION TIME 30 MINUTES

## INGREDIENTS

4 tbsp white balsamic vinegar

200 g / 7 oz / 1 ⅓ cups strawberries, sliced

1 lemon

50 g / 1 ¾ oz / ½ cup icing (confectioners') sugar

225 g / 8 oz / 1 cup Greek yoghurt

225 g / 8 oz / 1 cup whipped cream

## METHOD

- Pour the balsamic vinegar over the strawberries and leave to marinate for 25 minutes.

- Use a citrus zester to finely pare the lemon ring into strips and reserve for the garnish. Squeeze the lemon and mix the juice with the icing sugar to dissolve, then stir it into the yoghurt. Fold in the whipped cream.

- Divide the yoghurt mixture between 4 glasses and top with the marinated strawberries. Sprinkle with lemon zest and serve immediately.

**TOP TIP**

Replace the balsamic vinegar with orange liqueur for an adults-only treat.

# Spiced Fruit Salad

## REDIENTS

g / 7 oz / ¾ cup caster (superfine) sugar

nnamon stick

ar anise

omegranate, halved

ineapple, peeled and cut into chunks

ears, peeled, cored and cut into chunks

g / 5 ½ oz / 1 cup seedless red grapes

## METHOD

- Put the sugar and spices in a saucepan with 300 ml / ½ pint / 1 ¼ cups of water and stir over a medium heat to dissolve the sugar. Once the sugar has dissolved, stop stirring and let it boil for 8 minutes or until thick and syrupy.

- Hold the pomegranate halves over the pan and hit the backs with a wooden spoon to release the seeds. Stir them into the syrup with the rest of the fruit, then leave to cool and infuse for 20 minutes.

**TOP TIP**

Cinnamon ice cream makes a great accompaniment to this fruit salad.

# Poached Apricots with Honey and Rosemary

## METHOD

- Put the apricots in a saucepan with the apple juice, honey and rosemary.

- Cover and simmer gently for 5 minutes or until the apricots are soft, but still holding their shape. Serve warm or leave to cool before chilling.

**SERVES 4**

**PREPARATION TIME 5 MINUTES**

**COOKING TIME 5 MINUTES**

## INGREDIENTS

12 apricots, halved and stoned
100 ml / 3 ½ fl. oz / ½ cup apple juice
4 tbsp runny honey
1 tbsp rosemary leaves

**TOP TIP**
This recipe also works really well with peaches in place of the apricots.

# Chocolate and Walnut Pancakes

**SERVES 4**

**PREPARATION TIME 5 MINUTES**

**COOKING TIME 20 MINUTES**

## INGREDIENTS

200 g / 7 oz / 1 ⅓ cups plain (all purpose) flour

50 g / 1 ¾ oz / ½ cup unsweetened cocoa powder

1 tsp baking powder

2 large eggs

300 ml / 10 ½ fl. oz / 1 ¼ cups milk

2 tbsp butter

2 tbsp walnuts, chopped

## METHOD

- Mix the flour, cocoa and baking powder in a bowl and make a well in the centre. Break in the eggs and pour in the milk then use a whisk to gradually incorporate all of the flour from round the outside.

- Divide the butter between 4 mini frying pans and heat to melt, then whisk the butter into the batter. Put the buttered frying pans back over a low heat.

- Spoon the batter into the pans and cook for 2 minutes or until small bubbles start to appear on the surface. Turn the pancakes over with a spatula and cook the other side until golden brown and cooked through.

- Repeat until all the batter has been used, keeping the finished batches warm in a low oven. Pile the pancakes onto warm plates and sprinkle with walnuts.

**TOP TIP**
Try spreading the pancakes with chocolate spread and sprinkle with nuts.

# Baked Apples

**SERVES 4**

**PREPARATION TIME 5 MINUTES**

**COOKING TIME 25 MINUTES**

## INGREDIENTS

4 small Bramley apples

4 tbsp salted butter

4 tbsp light brown sugar

## METHOD

- Preheat the oven to 180°C (160°C fan) / 355F / gas 4.

- Use an apple corer to remove the apple cores, then sit them in a snug baking dish. Beat the butter and sugar together then pack the mixture into the cavities.

- Bake the apples for 25 minutes or until a skewer will slide in easily all the way to the centre.

**TOP TIP**

Serve the apples with a scoop of caramel ice cream for extra indulgence.

# Portuguese Custard Tarts

**MAKES 12**

**PREPARATION TIME 10 MINUTES**

**COOKING TIME 20 MINUTES**

## INGREDIENTS

- 375 g pack of ready-rolled, all-butter puff pastry
- 4 large egg yolks, beaten
- 50 g / 1 ¾ oz / ¼ cup caster (superfine) sugar
- 2 tsp cornflour (cornstarch)
- 175 ml / 8 fl. oz / ¾ cup whole milk
- 1 lemon, zest finely grated
- 1 tsp ground cinnamon

## METHOD

- Preheat the oven to 200°C (180°C fan) / 390F / gas 6.

- Unroll the pastry on a floured surface and cut out 12 circles with a pastry cutter.

- Use the circles to line a 12-hole cupcake tin.

- Mix the rest of the ingredients together in a jug, then pour it into the pastry cases.

- Transfer the tin to the oven and bake for 20 minutes or until the pastry is golden brown and cooked through underneath.

**TOP TIP**

Serve the tarts with vanilla flavoured whipped cream for an extra indulgent treat.

# Orange and Passion Fruit Verrines

## SERVES 4
## PREPARATION TIME 30 MINUTES

## INGREDIENTS

2 oranges

50 g / 1 ¾ oz / ½ cup icing (confectioners') sugar, sieved

450 g / 1 lb / 2 cups Greek yoghurt

4 passion fruit

150 g / 5 ½ oz / ⅔ cup coconut cake, cubed

## METHOD

- Use a vegetable peeler to pare 4 thin slices of orange zest and reserve for decoration. Slice the top and bottom off the oranges. Slice away the peel then cut out each individual segment, leaving the white pith behind like the pages of a book. Discard the pith.

- Fold the icing sugar into the yoghurt.

- Divide the orange segments between 4 glass bowls and top with the pulp and seeds from 2 of the passion fruit. Spoon over half of the yoghurt.

- Arrange the cake cubes on top, then spoon over the rest of the yoghurt and top with the rest of the passion fruit pulp. Garnish with the reserved orange zest.

**TOP TIP**

Replace the oranges with ruby grapefruit for a sharper flavour.

# INDEX